Touch Training for
Strength

Beth Rothenberg
Oscar Rothenberg

Human Kinetics

Library of Congress Cataloging-in-Publication Data

Rothenberg, Beth, 1942-
    Touch training for strength / Beth Rothenberg & Oscar Rothenberg.
      p. cm.
    Includes bibliographical references (p.) and index.
    ISBN 0-87322-437-X
    1. Physical education and training. 2. Muscle strength.
    3. Weight training. 4. Sensorimotor integration. I. Rothenberg, Oscar,
    1931-   . II. Title.
    GV711.5.R68   1995
    613.7'1--dc20   94-1605
                                                  CIP

Acquisitions Editor: Richard Frey, PhD; **Developmental Editor:** Holly Gilly; **Assistant Editors:** Anna Curry, Ed Giles, and Dawn Roselund; **Copyeditor:** John Wentworth; **Proofreader:** Susan Dove; **Indexer:** Joan K. Griffitts; **Typesetting and Layout:** Ruby Zimmerman; **Text Design:** Keith Blomberg; **Cover Design:** Jack Davis; **Interior Art:** Karen Kuchar; **Cover and Interior Photos:** Ronnie Ramos; **Models:** Nicole Bubis (cover), Carole Clarke, Jonathan Kei, and Craig Love (cover and interior); **Printer:** United Graphics

Printed in the United States of America   10 9 8 7 6 5 4 3 2

Human Kinetics
P.O. Box 5076, Champaign, IL 61825-5076
1-800-747-4457

Canada: Human Kinetics, Box 24040, Windsor, ON N8Y 4Y9
1-800-465-7301 (in Canada only)

Europe: Human Kinetics, P.O. Box IW14, Leeds LS16 6TR, England
(44) 532 781708

Australia: Human Kinetics, 2 Ingrid Street, Clapham 5062, South Australia
(08) 371 3755

New Zealand: Human Kinetics, P.O. Box 105-231, Auckland 1
(09) 309 2259

We dedicate this book to our sons, Erik and
Carl, to remind them to believe in themselves,
never give up, follow their dreams,
and marry nice girls.

CONTENTS

WELCOME TO SYSTEMATIC T.O.U.C.H. TRAINING^{SM}

Strength trainers have access to a host of high-tech machines that can produce rapid advances in muscle strength. As the machines have gotten better, exercisers have begun to rely on them more. While these advances have helped to improve performance and minimize injuries, we feel the current emphasis on technology has allowed exercisers to ignore the important role of the brain and the neuromuscular system in developing muscle strength and function.

We wrote this book specifically for strength and conditioning specialists, coaches, fitness instructors, and serious athletes. The book explains how to use the innate organization of the sensorimotor system of healthy exercisers to enhance the mental image of movement and to increase the force of muscle contractions. We explain the physiological and psychological basis of our training process while offering hands-on guidelines for using it. We believe you will find, as we have, that Systematic T.O.U.C.H. Training^{SM} (STT) enhances the effects of all other training methods, and that our step-by-step approach will help athletes reach peak performance and gain a competitive edge by maximizing muscle strength and improving concentration.

In chapter 1 we describe how STT began and explain how to use the technique to build strength and improve muscle function. We introduce the five basic benefits of STT and offer the opinions of distinguished athletes, coaches, and trainers who already use the system. The skin has the unique—but underdeveloped and underutilized—ability to process information from the external environment and from within the body. We emphasize the powerful influence that touch exerts on human behavior and its capacity to improve the mind–body connection during exercise.

No formal research into the value of touch as a strength training technique has been done; therefore, much of the evidence supporting the usefulness of touch is anecdotal. In chapter 2, however, we present an overview of the possible scientific and theoretical explanations for the success of touch training.

In chapter 3 we answer questions about how to touch, when to touch, and what speed and intensity of touch to use. We explore the power of "phantom fingers" to help improve muscle sequencing and coordination. We describe how STT can be used as a form of biofeedback and how it can be employed to either relax or stimulate a contraction.

Chapter 4 details our four-step procedure for incorporating STT into your weight training program. We provide helpful hints, such as the importance of rhythm, consistent touch cuing, and putting the exerciser in correct body alignment with touch.

In chapter 5 we classify skeletal muscles into three categories, discuss their characteristics, and present different methods for touching each during exercise. We present procedures to follow when exercising one of the muscles within each of the muscle groups. These procedures can then be applied to other muscles in the same category and to all possible exercises that could be performed by the muscle. The appendix expands on this chapter by explaining how to use STT with 23 other specific exercises.

Finally, in chapter 6 we discuss the future of STT and its potential for improving athletic and sport-related skills. We also explain how STT can be used to provide feedback and feedforward information to the athlete.

Read the book. Use the method. We think you'll be amazed that the ability to increase muscle strength and function and to improve coordination has always been, literally, right in the palm of your hand.

ACKNOWLEDGMENTS

Foremost among the many to whom we owe a debt of gratitude is our acquisitions editor, Richard Frey, PhD, who helped organize the text, suggested sources of research, and even conducted some of his own research into the neurophysiological basis of STT. His unfailing support and enthusiasm for the project inspired us to put forth our best efforts.

We must also extend a heartfelt thanks to our developmental editor, Holly Gilly, for her perseverance and professionalism and for her patience in allowing us to intrude so often on her precious family time with lengthy after-hours phone calls.

By the same token our appreciation also goes out to the entire staff of Human Kinetics and particularly to Keith Blomberg, our photography editor, whose technical skills helped save us time and avoid expensive mistakes. The sincerely warm, supportive, and friendly approach we encountered from everyone connected with the company was not at all what one would expect from a leading publishing house.

In researching this book we relied heavily on the resources and expertise of many individuals. Some made significant contributions merely by discussing with us their own areas of interest—generously sharing their technical knowledge and experience. Others helped solve problems by referring us to useful texts or other professionals in various scientific disciplines. Still others read and reread our manuscript, offering invaluable contributions and corrections. Among these gifted professionals we gratefully acknowledge Lynn Paul Taylor, RPT, a specialist in the development of treatment protocols; Stuart Rugg, PhD, chair of the Kinesiology Department and professor of anatomy and biomechanics, Occidental College; Mary Monroe, writer/editor; personal trainer Mary Lou Taylor; and coach Chris Frankel.

We are also indebted to the artistic eye and steady hand of Ronnie Ramos, whose carefully crafted photography enriches the book. Thanks are also due to our models, Carole Clarke, a registered nurse and triathlete, and Craig Love, a personal fitness trainer and kick boxer. Both are superb athletes and dedicated professionals. A special thanks to the Santa Monica Body Building Center for making its facilities available to us.

These acknowledgments would not be complete without mentioning Karen Kuchar, a talented artist who is responsible for the skillful illustrations, and Vail Romeyn, who never tired of retyping the many revisions of our manuscript. Vail came to us as a part-time typist and stayed to become a full-time friend.

Finally, to all of the wonderful clients who over the years so generously gave of their time, advice, and support: Thank you one and all. Without your help, confidence, and encouragement, STT could not have been developed.

Thank you Oscar for being my best friend, the love of my life, and the man who made all my dreams come true.

Thank you for believing in me and for the hours, weeks, and years it took to write this book.

I was truly blessed the day I found you.

Beth

A NOTE
TO THE READER

This book represents one of the more ambitious undertakings of a dynamic and loving marriage that has lasted 30 years. How my wife and I came to write it is described in some detail in the first chapter. It turned out to be a formidable task for both of us. Neither Beth's considerable knowledge nor my many years of practice in the medical-legal field equipped us to read and interpret the volumes of available scientific literature bearing upon so vast a topic as the sense of touch. We needed help.

Fortunately, we found precisely the help we needed when we were introduced to Dr. Michael Lacourse, an exercise scientist at California State University, Long Beach with expertise in motor behavior. Dr. Lacourse carefully read the first draft of our manuscript. To our delight, he validated many of our initial impressions and provided needed encouragement. He continued to take a keen interest in the project and offered welcome corrections, criticisms, and suggestions. In the succeeding months, he gathered the results of scientific studies conducted at various universities around the world and explained to us how they tended to substantiate our conclusions. Dr. Lacourse is the kind of collaborator authors look for but seldom find. Beth and I are sincerely grateful for the opportunity to work with him. Without his knowledge, talent, and dedication, this book would never have come to print.

We have chosen to present the material that follows primarily in Beth's voice to fully utilize her point of view as a veteran personal trainer with years of experience in developing the Systematic T.O.U.C.H. training technique.

Oscar Rothenberg

CHAPTER One

WHAT IS SYSTEMATIC T.O.U.C.H. TRAINING^{SM}?

> Forward, forward let us range,
> Let the great world spin forever
> down the ringing grooves of change.
>
> Alfred, Lord Tennyson (1842)

Early in my career as a personal fitness trainer, I found it curious that some clients quickly achieved significant, visible improvements in strength and muscle tone, while others, even after training faithfully for many months, reported that they could scarcely feel the target muscle working during exercise. It seemed only natural for me to place my hands over their muscles to evaluate the strength of the contraction. In doing so, I found I could often detect the reasons for their limited progress. Many of these clients were relying on incorrect muscle groups to do most of the work during the movement. For example, they would initiate the lift in a bent-over row with the arms instead of with the muscles of the back. During a lateral deltoid raise they would use the trapezius more than the deltoid. Most of my clients lacked a basic understanding of the location and shape of the target muscle, so I would sometimes outline its boundaries with my forefinger, enabling the exerciser to form a clear mental picture of the muscle that should be contracted.

Opening the Lines of Communication Between Mind and Muscle

Palpating and outlining the muscles helped me collect and convey a great deal of valuable information, and it became a regular part of my training program. However, other frustrating obstacles soon arose. Some clients lacked the necessary kinesthetic awareness to follow directions even after the muscle had been outlined and the exact location of the desired contraction identified. Other clients seemed unable to focus on the movement, as if they were not paying attention.

I wanted to open up the lines of communication between the mind and the body to better train the muscle. Verbal explanations and visualization techniques often were not enough. So I began to augment them by touching the skin over the muscle to focus the client's attention.

Most clients seemed to respond favorably to the additional sensory input. They not only improved their focus during training but also better understood what I had been trying so hard to explain. When verbal cuing alone proved insufficient, touching seemed to provide a new and effective "language." Later on, I found it helpful to have clients touch my muscles as I demonstrated an exercise. This way they experienced just how a properly exercised muscle should feel through a full range of motion. Touching gave both exerciser and trainer instant feedback.

Training by touch provided a host of additional benefits. For example, I discovered that with the proper touch I could teach clients who "cheated" or "muscled" their way through an exercise to eliminate tension in "helper" muscles, which enabled them to work the involved muscles more effectively, decrease fatigue, and avoid injury.

Because they remained focused during exercise sessions, my clients were able to work out more efficiently in that they worked harder for shorter periods of time. I even found that strength training clients made rapid strides using lighter weights and that the effect of touch was the same whether administered to bare skin or over light clothing. Although I was excited by my success, I did not consider my technique innovative. In fact, during my first few years of experimenting with the touch method I wrongly assumed that all trainers used this simple technique to monitor muscle tension and focus the attention of their clients.

Some Puzzling Questions

Many years passed before I began to suspect that my touch technique was doing more than focusing attention. I discovered that some of my clients were able to continue to squeeze out repetitions even after they thought their strength was totally spent. I wondered if my technique was somehow delaying the onset of muscle fatigue. Was it possible that palpating key points on the skin in some way stimulated the contraction of additional muscle fibers and generated renewed strength within the muscle? If so, I wondered how deep the pressure should be in order to increase the force of the contraction. Would the magnitude be the same for everyone? And where, when, and how often should I use touch during a training session? These were questions that needed answering before I could understand and improve my technique.

Pursuing the Answers

I knew I could answer these questions only through trial and error. There were no texts to use as a reference nor any known research on the use of touch as a formal training technique. Fortunately, I was working with a large group of healthy, inquisitive clients willing to take time from their regular workouts to report their every reaction and response. I carefully noted the training effects on the clients and documented their impressions. As I perfected my method, my clients experienced a corresponding increase in strength and improved muscle function.

Lawyer Joins Trainer—A Perfect Team

In the winter of 1988 I asked my husband, Oscar, to join me in pursuit of a scientific explanation for the apparent success of my technique. Reluctantly at first and with a lawyer's typical skepticism, he agreed to help me collect and study data that was scattered about in the UCLA Biomedical Library. After weeks of research, what impressed us most was not so much what we found in the literature but what we did not find. We were unable to locate a single work that described or used specific patterns of touch to isolate or stimulate muscle groups in healthy, exercising individuals. The use of muscle stimulation, facilitated by sensory input, seemed to be the exclusive province of the physical therapist and restricted to patients suffering from disease or injury of the neuromuscular system.

Given our limited scientific training, Oscar and I followed many false paths and reached more than our share of dead ends. Because our careers occupied most of our time, we initially worked only on weekends. We consulted exercise physiologists, physical therapists, biomechanists, and neurophysiologists. Some were encouraging, others dubious, but almost all were as fascinated with the idea of touch training as we were. Our most enthusiastic support came from professionals with a strong background in motor learning. In the end, neither of us could avoid becoming quite absorbed in the effort. Eventually, we identified the factors that we now believe constitute the anatomical and neurophysiological basis of touch training and went on to systematize these techniques for easy study by others—hence the name, systematic touch training (STT).

Five Benefits of Systematic T.O.U.C.H. Training^{SM}

While formulating the components of the system, we recognized these five basic benefits:

- STT redirects the focus of the exerciser's attention toward the target muscle(s).
- STT provides a form of biofeedback to the brain.
- STT facilitates a muscle contraction.
- STT enables the trainer to evaluate for muscle tension and muscle imbalances during exercise.
- STT helps eliminate tension in those muscles that are inappropriate for a given exercise.

And that, in short, was how STT began. The system came to exist because I felt challenged to find a way to train those clients unable to fully benefit from verbal explanations or visual demonstrations. STT has since proved to be an extremely versatile tool that is adaptable to a wide range of training styles.

Your own challenge as a trainer or coach is to design effective programs that meet today's ever-increasing health, fitness, and athletic objectives. Our simple techniques can help the strength training professional achieve these goals while providing a training edge.

WHAT DO LEADING PROFESSIONALS SAY ABOUT STT?

Here are just a few of the comments of leading coaches, trainers, and elite athletes who have experimented with STT.

"This is a viable technique. It is exceptionally useful for evaluation of my athletes as it gives me immediate feedback about problem areas. There are machines that measure muscle imbalance, but I tend to use them more for the initial assessment and periodic testing than for spot-checking. Your hands-on evaluation techniques are instant and surprisingly accurate. Both coach and athlete get immediate feedback."

John Arce
Head Strength and Conditioning Coach,Purdue University; trainer of Olympic champions in track and field, swimming; trainer of six NCAA championship teams; and trainer of professional athletes

"Touching is the missing link between visual imagery and body mechanics. It is the mind–body connection that everyone is looking for. I see the improvement. It enhances the ability of the athlete to perform proper muscle sequencing patterns. The cues that coaches use typically are visual and audi-tory. What this technique provides is an additional cue that may stimulate the proper response which could perhaps be missing or may need to be in-cluded to more finely tune the technical process or execution. For example, with regard to sprint me-chanics, it is a more specific method for isolating or placing emphasis on the prime mover. I can instruct the athlete to focus on the muscle that they should be using, and they are able to use it during the move-ment. I've also used it to coach high jumpers and throwers. It is one more link in drawing their attention to the movement. I'm using it more and more all the time."

Allan Hanckel
President, Athleticorp, *involved in the training of elite athletes, such as Jackie Joyner-Kersee, André Phillips, Trish Porter, Doug Nordquist, members of the Los Angeles Raiders, including Howie Long, and Heismann Trophy-winner Tim Brown*

"I'm very impressed with this new training tool. Systematic touch training techniques facilitate the connection between mind and body, which better enables an athlete to tune in to a specific exercise. I am especially excited about the possibilities of using STT with young athletes who in general have a harder time making that connection. I can also see where it would be extremely helpful when teaching running technique, weightlifting, and individual track-and-field events. The possibilities of using STT to prevent injuries and to help athletes retrain injured muscles seem endless."

Pam Spencer Marquez
Three-time Olympic high jumper, former American record holder, coach of Women's World Cup and Olympic Festival track-and-field teams

"Some people use the wrong muscles no matter how many times I tell them to do it right. This touching helps them to stay focused and train correctly. Some people don't listen when you talk to them, but they listen when you touch."

George Pipasik
Four-time titleholder, "Mr. Czechoslovakia," personal trainer of Dolph Lundgren, Sugar Ray Leonard, Sylvester Stallone, Sally Field, Julianne Philipps, Marsha Mason, and other celebrities

"It is a totally different way of strength training. When I use the touch technique, my clients are better able to overcome fatigue and squeeze out more repetitions. Furthermore, many clients cannot relax a muscle when asked to do so, but adding touch to the verbal instruction helps them release the tension."

Rebecca Eastman
Personal fitness trainer for 15 years and author of Full Circle Fitness

"This new technique keeps me and my clients mentally sharp. I find that even if I am training them with lighter weights I seem to get more work out of them. The touch technique makes you feel you are working with the weights instead of working against them. My clients are fascinated with this technique. It also builds a strong wall around me and my client in a crowded gym. I can keep them totally focused with touch. Touching enhances verbal cues that the athletes have difficulty picking up."

Shannon Madill
Personal fitness trainer for 10 years, stuntwoman, and sports coach

Why Is the Method So Effective?

STT is effective because it relies on an underused, fundamental human sense. It can enhance all the other methods currently in use. Conventional methods for isolating muscle groups include mental imagery, verbal commands, and use of various types of machinery. These are all valid and useful methods, but each can be enhanced by STT.

The beauty of our touch training method is that it is simple to learn. However, during our review of the scientific literature, we found that the reasons it works are not so simple. There are still many unanswered questions about the mind–body connection. We'll discuss possible explanations in chapter 2. First, let's look at some basic facts about reflexes, skin receptors, and the skin's communication with the neuromuscular system.

Touching Makes Sense

If priority of sensation alone were to be regarded, the sense of touch might deserve to be considered the most important; as it must have been exercised long before birth, and it is probably the very feeling with which sentient life begins.
L.E. Krueger

The *skin* is a sensory receptor and, like our eyes and ears, continually scans for new and important information. However, compared to our other receptors, the skin's pressure receptors receive relatively little stimulation. Because they are under-stimulated and underutilized, they operate in a constant state of heightened sensitivity. When the skin is touched, sensory information is swiftly processed, providing the brain with a wealth of information.

Does Touch Influence Behavior?

Our sense of touch has been called the "mother of the senses" and is the earliest to develop in the human embryo. Upon birth, receptors in the skin immediately transmit sensations of heat, cold, touch, pain, and overall comfort. As infants are cuddled, carried, hugged, and stroked, each of these acts stimulates the skin and helps develop the mind–body connection. However, as years pass we tend to withdraw from the sense of touch and from being touched.

Ashley Montagu recognized the importance of touch and its role in developing the mind–body connection. He published his findings in his celebrated book, *Touching: The Human Significance of the Skin* (now in its third edition). Montagu explored the effect of touching, and of *not* touching, on human behavior and proposed that the sensation of touch be regarded as a basic human need. He argued that people cannot survive without skin stimulation—whether that stimulation comes from other people, from water pouring over our skin in the shower, or even from the touch of clothing. The need to touch and be touched exerts a significant influence on our behavior.

Some of our first movements outside the womb result from skin stimulation. Touching an infant's cheek, for instance, results in a turn of the infant's head toward the touch (*rooting reflex*). If you press your finger into the palm of an infant's hand, it will squeeze it (*palmar grasp reflex*). Touching the sole of an infant's foot results in a prehensile (grasping) response of the foot (*plantar grasp reflex*). Touching one side of the back near the infant's spine will cause the infant to bend toward that side. These inborn reactions to touch are evidence that when the skin is touched in a specific way, a muscle (or a group of muscles) contracts reflexively.

Despite its power, touch is used only selectively in communication. Among friends and the people we love, touch is the language of intimacy, but among strangers, it often arouses self-consciousness or suspicion. The handshake and the pat on the back are symbolic gestures in our culture, but any other touch from a stranger often leads to uncertainty about the intended message. Consequently, many of us are reluctant to touch and choose to express ourselves verbally or visually instead.

What's the Sense in Having Skin?

A general rule of neurology is that the size of a specific area of the brain relates to the number of functions the area performs. Skin receptors are well represented in the brain. And even the nerves in the spinal cord that conduct Morse code–like messages from the skin are usually larger than those associated with the other senses.

So, the skin's relative importance in providing sensory information to the brain is evidenced by the large area of sensory cortex devoted to the skin. In 1980, a team of researchers headed by Michael Merzenich, a neurophysiologist, reported that the portion of the brain associated with touch can change (enlarge) through repetitive stimulation of the skin, suggesting that the map of the brain can be altered by stimulating a specific area of the skin. As the part of the brain associated with touch enlarges, connections can be established with the nerves that extend from the brain to the muscles, thereby improving the mind–body connection.

There are several types of receptors in the skin, each responsible for detecting a unique stimulus (pressure, temperature, or pain). The density of these receptors differs for various body parts. For example, the palm of your hand has a much greater density of receptors than the back of your leg. This is true for functional reasons, as the hands are involved in manipulating small objects and need to be sensitive, whereas the back of the leg does not need such sensitivity. The greater an area's density of receptors, the more detailed the information that can be sent to the brain through touch.

Once a skin receptor has been stimulated through touch, the nerve impulse travels a complex and diffuse path to the brain. The first stop is the spinal cord. Each of the 30 segments of the spinal cord is responsible for collecting sensations from a different area of the skin. Once the impulse arrives at the spinal cord, it travels to the brain so that the touch is perceived, and then to other segments of the spinal cord to modify movements, often reflexively. After leaving the spinal cord, the impulse travels to various structures in the brain, to the thalamus, and finally to the somatosensory cortex, where the information from the skin combines with input from the eyes, ears, tongue, and nose to provide an overall perception.

Imagine the World on the Tip of Your Finger!

Skin stimulation is now being used as a means of helping the blind to read. Several years ago, physiological psychologist Bach-y-Rita developed a device for the blind that stimulated the skin with vibrating pins to create images on the upper back. He found that the impression created was similar to seeing the image.

STT's potential for producing a mental picture can be demonstrated by stimulating the skin with different patterns of touch. When these patterns resemble those received from vision, it is possible that the information from the skin could be used for developing mental pictures for producing certain types of movements. For example, we can help an exerciser isolate a particular muscle by running a finger on the skin along the muscle boundary. Developing a mental picture of the muscle helps the exerciser in the future when he or she tries to remember which muscle to contract and its proper sequence of contraction during an exercise. At this point we can begin to see how STT might be useful in improving performance in sport. We'll discuss such applications in chapter 6.

Stimulation of the skin may also serve as a cue for guiding motor responses. Used as a source of feedback, a touch to the skin can guide a person's movement in the same way that visually tracking the flight of a baseball can guide the swing of a baseball bat. Upon sensing the location of a touch on the skin, a person can then focus on contracting the muscle that lies directly below the skin at that location. For example, when an exerciser is performing a biceps curl, walking your fingers along his or her biceps guides the movement. Touching the skin lets the person know which body part should be contracting. It is not surprising, then, that STT can improve the mind–body connection during exercise.

Summary

Experimentation with STT began over 20 years ago in an effort to help exercisers avoid using incorrect muscle groups and to focus their attention on the movement. The technique has since developed into a useful method for exercisers and trainers to improve the connection between the mind and the body. In our experience, STT helps to eliminate tension in inappropriate muscles, facilitate a muscle contraction, delay the effects of muscle fatigue, isolate the target muscle, detect muscle imbalances, and provide instant feedback about problem areas. In later chapters we will provide step-by-step procedures for applying STT principles. First, however, we cannot resist offering some possible explanations for why the technique is so successful.

CHAPTER Two

WHY DOES STT WORK?

We dance 'round the ring and suppose,
but the secret sits in the middle and knows.

Robert Frost (1942)

There exists no single unifying theory that explains why STT works. Even after 20 years of using my touch training technique, I am still uncertain which of several possible mechanisms accounts for its success. Scientists have not yet provided us with a sufficient understanding of the nervous system to offer a complete explanation. Until a controlled and definitive study employing the scientific method is conducted, we are limited to offering our own thoughts and tentative conclusions. Our aim is to provoke your interest and curiosity and invite you to explore further the nature of this phenomenon.

We believe that repeated touch during a weight training session leads to effective and efficient gains in strength through improved muscular function and enhanced performance. We are led to these conclusions by anecdotal reports from colleagues, evidence from our review of the literature, and my work with athletes and other strength and conditioning enthusiasts. Our evidence centers on some well-known scientific facts relative to sensorimotor reflexes, muscle fiber recruitment, selective attention, arousal–performance relationships, and pain attenuation principles. We invite you to explore with us some of these interesting theories.

Increased Muscle Strength Through Improved Muscle Function?

Traditionally, strength gains are thought to be accompanied by muscle hypertrophy—bigger is stronger. However, according to the Canadian muscle physiologist Digby Sale, strength is also increased by improving muscle function through several neural adaptations that occur as a result of strength training. According to Sale, these changes precede any increase in muscle size.

Muscle function refers to the efficiency and coordination of movements, including those used to perform exercises and sport-related skills. Muscle function improves because weight training stimulates numerous neurological adaptations that lead to improved coordination and efficiency among agonists, antagonists, synergists, and stabilizer muscles. It is not uncommon for a beginning weightlifter to show improvement in strength between the first and second training sessions with no accompanying hypertrophy.

There are three ways that STT may increase strength by improving muscle function. First, it may stimulate sensorimotor reflexes. Second, it may change the recruitment order of motor units. And third, it may improve the coordination of muscle contraction sequences among agonists, antagonists, and synergistic muscles.

Many scientists believe that the size of a muscle can be increased by frequent electrical stimulation of the nerve that innervates it. These electrical signals produce a chemical response that stimulates growth. Stimulation can originate from several sources, including the brain and various sensory receptors. Ultimately, however, they all converge in the spinal cord and connect with the nerve that travels to a set of fibers within the muscle. This nerve is referred to as the *final common pathway*. If the frequency of electrical signals sent along the final common path can somehow be increased, or if the number of excited motor units is increased, growth of the muscle fibers will be enhanced.

Stimulating Sensorimotor Reflexes

Based on our review of the scientific literature, we believe that the complex interconnections between the skin, nervous system, and muscles can be exploited to increase electrical stimulation to the muscle and thereby increase the magnitude of the muscle contraction. In effect, touching the skin over a muscle while the muscle is contracting produces a reflexive action that ultimately leads to the recruitment of muscle fibers that supplement the fibers already contracting voluntarily.

This phenomenon occurs because of the way the human nervous system is organized. When we use this natural organization to our advantage, we can increase the amount of tension produced by a muscle during a contraction. Physical therapists have used these methods for years. In fact, STT, to some extent, is related to the reflex-based methods of proprioceptive neuromuscular facilitation (PNF), or more specifically, to the technique of manual contact traditionally used by physical therapists during the rehabilitation of victims of stroke, disease, or injury to the neuromuscular system.

Some methods of manual contact were developed by Margaret Rood at the University of Southern California during the early 1960s. She advocated the use of specific patterns of touch to excite the central nervous system and reestablish injured or destroyed neural pathways. With recent technological advances in modalities and equipment, Rood's simple techniques are now rarely used or even unheard of. Consequently, the methods have never achieved recognition outside the realm of physical therapy and have been restricted to use with "unhealthy" persons. STT, however, is designed for *healthy* exercising individuals who wish to improve strength or skill or reshape their bodies. Both methods exploit the neuromuscular system to improve muscle strength.

How Does STT Initiate a Reflexive Contraction?   In response to a touch, electrical impulses are sent to the spinal cord, from where they may travel in two general directions: to the brain or to the nerves connecting to a unique muscle receptor beneath the touched skin. If the touch is administered properly, a reflexive contraction of the muscle below the surface of the touched skin can result. This happens because of the singular structure of a sensory receptor called the *muscle spindle*. The cigar-shaped muscle spindle is located parallel to the muscle fibers and responds to the rate of stretch of the muscle. When the muscle spindle detects a stretch, a stimulus is generated and sent to the spinal cord, which, in turn, can lead to a reflexive contraction.

With STT, however, we are not required to stretch a muscle to produce a reflexive muscle contraction. Fortunately, the sensitivity of the spindle may also be controlled by the brain or influences from other parts of the nervous system, such as the skin.

Within the capsule of the muscle spindle are two small fibers called *intrafusal* muscle fibers. Physiologist K.-E. Hagbarth has shown with animals that by exciting the receptors of the skin it is possible to stimulate a contraction of the intrafusal fibers that, in turn, elicits a reflexive contraction of the muscle—the same as if the muscle had actually been stretched. Scientists call this mechanism *facilitation*.

The noted neurophysiologist Richard Stein has studied how the strength of ongoing movements, such as a biceps curl or a leg extension, can be modified by a reflex. He found that a stimulus, such as a touch, can modify the sensitivity of the reflex so that even a light touch can lead to a reflexive excitation. He suggests that this innate ability has important functional and perhaps even evolutionary significance. For our purposes, however, we see it as a mechanism that should be developed and exploited to improve the strength and function of a muscle.

Opening Neural Connections Between the Brain and the Muscle.   Because this effect occurs only reflexively, it would seem that the skin would have to be touched during each muscle contraction for any benefit to result. We have found that this is not true. Repeatedly touching the muscle during contractions seems to result in motor learning. In other words, the connections between the sensory and motor nerves established as a result of touching may connect with the neural networks of the brain and spinal cord that control voluntary movement. During subsequent muscle contractions, the reflexive activity would be activated automatically, resulting in greater overall muscle strength.

As the muscles involved in an exercise become educated through repeated use of STT, we believe neural connections between the brain and the muscle, as well as between different muscles, are established. Scientists are still uncertain whether touching actually creates new neural connections or stimulates underutilized or dormant ones. But if we are correct, the movement is learned and functions automatically. Therefore, it would not be necessary to use STT during each repetition. In fact, using STT during each repetition may develop a dependency between you and your exerciser leading to possible regression to previous incorrect technique in your absence. Hence, only the occasional use of STT is recommended to maintain these new or revitalized neural connections.

Changing the Order of Muscle Fiber Recruitment

The second way that STT can lead directly to improved strength through improved function is by a change in the recruitment order of muscle fibers. The functional unit of the muscle is the motor unit, and it is made up of two parts— a motoneuron and the muscle fibers that it innervates. According to John Basmajian and Carlo DeLuca, two prominent muscle physiologists, an increase in muscle force during a single contraction results from either recruiting additional motor units or from increasing the frequency at which nerve impulses are sent to the muscle. Although they do not know precisely how these two processes work together, they believe that in many muscles the initial increase in force likely results from increasing the number of contracting motor units.

This occurs in a specific order (size principle). First the small motor units are recruited, followed by units of intermediate size and then finally the largest motor units. When the muscle begins to relax, the units are derecruited in reverse order. Consequently, the small units work the entire time that a muscle is contracted, whereas the large units contract only for a relatively short time. This means that when muscles are contracting less than maximally, many of the larger motor units are not activated.

Giving the Muscle a Boost.   In 1977 a team of neurophysiologists demonstrated that the order of muscle fiber recruitment could be changed by stimulating the receptors in the skin overlying the muscle. Then in 1991 Gary Kamen and his colleagues conducted research at Boston University that confirmed that when the skin over a small muscle is stimulated, the large fibers of the muscle are recruited more rapidly than when the skin is not stimulated. Based on this evidence, we believe that using STT can develop a new recruitment order in which the middle- and large-sized muscle fibers are recruited earlier than normal (size principle). Because the middle- and large-sized fibers are fast-twitch ones, this new order might yield a more powerful muscle contraction.

Only Skin Deep.   Bear in mind that we are trying to stimulate the skin receptors and not the muscle receptors. Applying deep pressure to the muscle during the contraction will not increase tension but, instead, will cause the muscle to stretch. It is not our desire to stretch the muscle. We are trying to excite the central nervous system to facilitate a stronger contraction and to develop neural connections.

Improving Coordination

STT may increase strength and improve muscle function by providing sensory feedback to enhance muscular coordination. For example, there is an optimal technique for performing each weight training exercise. Each muscle involved in the movement must contract in a definite sequence and to a specific magnitude. Deviating from this could lead to incorrect muscle development and even to injury. You might view STT as a means of improving motor learning in that touch gives feedback to the exerciser to use in modifying the patterns of muscle contractions.

This book assumes that readers have adequate knowledge to correctly teach these exercises. To use STT correctly you must know which muscles to use in each exercise and their approximate sequence of contraction. For those who need a review of basic anatomy and kinesiology, there are several excellent books available (see Bibliography).

Increased Muscle Strength Through Improved Performance?

We believe that STT leads to improved muscle strength by enhancing performance during the training session. First, it refocuses your exerciser's attention on the target muscle (selective attention); second, it arouses or excites the central nervous system; and third, it may attenuate pain caused by muscle fatigue. Let's examine each of these theories in greater detail.

Focusing Attention

We have all been told by teachers to "pay attention to your work." What they really mean is to concentrate or *focus* on our work. According to UCLA psychologist Richard Schmidt, scientific research has demonstrated that our focus of attention is limited to one stimulus at a time. This theory is called *selective attention*. One such stimulus on which we can direct our focus is a touch. Touch allows increased processing of the selected information and helps us ignore all of the other information competing for our attention. It enables information from a source (the skin) to travel along a neural pathway to higher brain centers.

When a touch occurs, the exerciser concentrates on the location of the touch. With information about where the contraction should occur, he or she is better able to direct energy toward contracting the muscle at that location. During weight training, for example, the center of attention should be on moving the resistance. This is a relatively broad focus. Consequently, we are unable to focus our attention on contracting any single muscle. Because we are concentrating on the overall movement, it is possible that some muscles may not be contracting maximally or contributing their fair share to the exercise. When the skin is touched, as in STT, the focus of attention is on the muscle that underlies the skin at that location, enabling one to direct energy toward contracting that muscle. This works especially well if the exerciser is not frequently touched. A sudden, unexpected touch leads to a rapid switching of attention to the location of the touch. The exerciser will stop daydreaming and focus on the stimulation. However, if the exerciser is repeatedly touched in the same way, he or she may become accustomed to the touch and not respond as quickly or intensely. Psychologists call this process *habituation*, and it is a process we try to avoid.

Exciting the Brain

Touching arouses and excites the brain and nervous system. *Arousal* is defined as the level of activity in the central nervous system. Increased arousal means that there is an elevated level of neural and biochemical activity; low arousal means that there is relatively little activity, such as during sleep. The part of the brain responsible for controlling arousal receives information from the sensory receptors and from the cerebrum. A touch to the skin increases arousal, and the brain refocuses its attention from wherever it was (e.g., daydreaming) to the location of the touch.

Eighty-six years ago, the psychologists Yerkes and Dodson discovered that some motor skills are performed maximally only when a certain level of arousal is attained. Any other level of arousal results in a less than maximal performance. It is interesting to note that the optimal level of arousal is different for each motor skill. When lifting weights, higher levels of arousal often enable some exercisers to lift more weight. Hence, it seems fair to suggest that touching can lead to improved strength just by increasing overall arousal and focusing attention to the muscles where energy is needed.

Beating the Pain to the Brain

Another interesting theory may help explain acute strength improvement as a consequence of *cutaneous stimulation*. It has been suggested that cutaneous stimulation produces an increase in the strength of a muscle contraction by somehow inhibiting the transmission of impulses from pain receptors (i.e., free nerve endings). An example would be the pain that develops from the buildup of lactic acid in the muscle during exercise. The pain receptors synapse on small-diameter sensory nerves that conduct impulses at approximately 45 miles an hour. Cutaneous receptors, however, are connected to relatively large-diameter sensory nerves that allow signals to travel at speeds up to 225 miles an hour. Obviously, cutaneous signals arrive at the central nervous system much faster than pain signals. There are classic studies dating as early as the 1960s by Melzack and Wall that indicate that pain impulses ascending to the brain can be suppressed by cutaneous stimulation. Basically, the theory, named the gate-control theory, is that the faster-arriving cutaneous signals prevent the slower-arriving pain signals from reaching consciousness.

Cutaneous stimulation, therefore, might cause increases in the strength of muscular contractions during exercise by suppressing some of the pain from muscle fatigue. This is also a plausible explanation for why many of my clients who think they have reached their fatigue or pain point can suddenly do additional repetitions as soon as the skin over the muscle is touched.

Summary

Because touch training is so new and has yet to undergo the scrutiny of formal scientific investigation, we are not yet certain what causes the phenomenon. However, credible evidence rooted in well-known and proven scientific principles exists to justify our faith in its efficacy.

So far, we have identified six possible explanations for the success of STT:

- STT may recruit additional motor units through a reflexive muscle contraction.
- STT may change the order of muscle fiber recruitment.
- STT may improve intermuscular coordination.
- STT may focus attention on a specific muscle or muscle group.
- STT may increase general neural activity to a muscle during a contraction.
- STT may attenuate the pain that occurs with muscle fatigue.

Any or all of these explanations might be behind the success we've had with STT. It is also possible that the best explanation has yet to be discovered. In any case, there is no denying the benefits my exercisers have attained through our touch technique. In the next chapter we'll show you how to incorporate STT into your program designs.

CHAPTER Three

TOUCH THIS WAY!

How to Use STT: Part I

> No theory is good except on condition
> that one use it to go beyond.
>
> André Gide (1918)

Now that you understand more about the concept of touch training and its significance, we will show you how to incorporate STT into your repertoire of training methods. In this and the following two chapters, we will concentrate on the "how-to" of using STT. Here we will start by describing and illustrating the seven different STT methods of touch. Then we will discuss

- who to touch,
- when to touch,
- how often to touch,
- how hard to touch, and
- how fast to touch.

Finally, we will explore four of the most frequently asked questions about the practical uses of STT.

For clarity, from this point on we will refer to the person who is being touched as the *exerciser* and the person who is doing the touching as the *trainer*. (We do not mean to suggest that these methods are restricted to only trainers!) Also, we will use the descriptions *touching the muscle* and *touching the skin over the muscle* interchangeably. When we speak of touching the skin over the muscle we do not mean to imply that you need to touch the skin directly. The methods discussed here are equally effective when the touch is felt through light clothing, such as T-shirts, sweatshirts, or pants.

The Seven Methods of Touch

To facilitate a muscle contraction, we have developed a variety of stroking and touch techniques. Each of these techniques serves a specific purpose and will elicit a slightly different response. The techniques may have different effects on the motoneurons that innervate the muscle and the nerves that ascend to the brain because each method stimulates a different combination of receptors. The reason for these various effects remains unknown.

The methods we'll discuss here include *maintained touch, stroking, palpation/squeeze, walking, cupping,* and *knife-edge.* Each of these methods is summarized in Table 3.1. We suggest that you read the discussion for each method several times and then refer to the table as needed. Another technique mentioned in the table, *phantom fingers,* has a unique purpose and will be discussed last.

Maintained Touch

We'll discuss maintained touch first because it is usually the first method used during the exercise session and is the primary method to use for evaluation. The method is quite simple and requires only that you place your hand flat or contoured against the surface of the skin above the contracting muscle.

Table 3.1
Methods of Touching

Method	Evaluation	Stimulation	Relaxation	Function			
				Gives direction to contraction	Focuses attention	For large muscle groups	For small muscle groups
Maintained touch	✓	—	✓	—	✓		✓
Stroking	—	✓	✓	✓	✓	✓	✓
Palpation/ squeeze	—	✓	✓	—	✓	✓	✓
Walking	—	✓	—	✓	✓	✓	✓
Cupping	✓	✓	—	—	✓	—	✓
Knife-edge	—	✓	—	✓	✓	✓	✓
Phantom fingers	—	✓	—	✓	✓	✓	✓

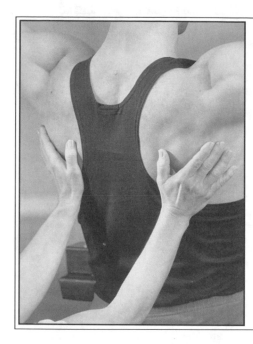

■ *3.1 The maintained touch hand position requires a flat or contoured hand.*

You may use your entire hand or any number of fingers (see Figure 3.1).

There are three reasons to use this method. First, it is used to evaluate the degree to which a specific muscle or area of a muscle is generating tension during a contraction (see Figure 3.2). Based on this information you can verbally instruct the exerciser to increase tension in that area of the muscle, or you can use another of the methods to further stimulate the contraction. Evaluation is not particularly difficult, but you should anticipate that it will take some practice and familiarity with your exercisers before you can accurately and consistently determine whether they are exerting all or part of their maximal strength.

Second, use maintained touch to help your exercisers eliminate tension in muscles that they are using inappropriately.

Finally, a third reason for using maintained touch is to provide information to your exercisers about the exact muscle to concentrate on during the exercise. This is usually done both before and during the contraction. Maintaining the position of your hand on the muscle, slowly move your hand back and

3.2 *Maintained touch can be used to evaluate a muscle during a contraction. Here the trainer has asked the exerciser to complete one repetition while she determines whether the movement originated with the latissimus.*

forth (as if your hand were shivering) for about 2 seconds. Moving your hand is necessary because the receptors of the skin tend to adjust quickly to a constant touch, and after a short time your exerciser would not even be aware of your touch. (For a demonstration of this, have someone touch you at a location you cannot see and then focus on what happens to the sensation over a brief time.) Remember—this shivering movement should not be used if the sole reason for the maintained touch is to provide you (the trainer) with information during the evaluation.

Stroking

Stroking (Figure 3.3) is similar to maintained touch in that you may use the entire hand or any number of fingers. When stroking, do not use a shivering-like movement but, instead, drag the fingers along the surface of the skin in the direction of the muscle pull. The motion is similar to petting a cat except that it is focused on either a single muscle or a discrete area of a muscle. Stroking is different from maintained touch in that it

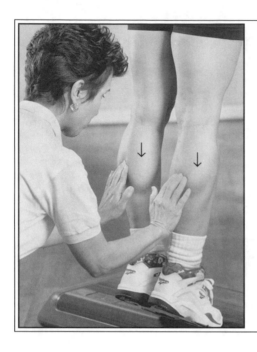

■ *3.3 The stroking technique hand position—stroke a muscle in the direction of its pull while depressing the skin.*

informs the exerciser about the *direction* the contraction should follow. In addition, it is used to stimulate a muscle contraction. You should pace your stroking movements a fraction of a second ahead of the exerciser's own contraction and drag the muscle into action.

The method is very simple. Slightly depress the skin surface with one or more fingers and stroke in the direction of the muscle pull. This movement stimulates the skin receptors and then allows them to recover after the touch passes over the area. How many fingers you use depends on the size of your hand and the surface area of your exerciser's muscle. Stroking requires you to repeatedly move your fingers in the overall direction of the muscle pull.

The direction is always the same as the contraction. If the contraction is concentric, stroke from the distal insertion to the proximal insertion. Conversely, if the contraction is eccentric, stroke from the proximal insertion to the distal insertion. As it is not necessary to depress the skin deeply, this method should not be painful. Remember—you are stimulating the muscle by using the receptors of the skin, not the receptors in the muscle. There is no reason to apply deep pressure, as this will not result in a stronger contraction. In fact, deep pressure could result in muscle relaxation in some instances.

Palpation/Squeeze

The palpation/squeeze method is either a palpating or a pincer-like movement and is appropriate for stimulating a muscle during contraction. The method is often employed to stimulate what I call "dead spots" in the muscle (areas with little or no muscle activity). In other words, if you use maintained touch to evaluate a muscle and you locate a specific area that does not seem to be involved in the contraction, you should use this method (with one, two, or three fingers) to stimulate that specific portion of the muscle. This technique provides feedback to your exerciser about which part of the muscle needs to be contracted.

The basic palpation technique varies depending on the number of fingers you use during the touch. One to three fingers are appropriate with relatively small muscles, such as the biceps and triceps, whereas two or more fingers should be employed with the larger muscles, such as the gluteus maximus, latissimus, and the quadriceps (see Figure 3.4). The reason to use two or more fingers with larger muscles is that the skin covering larger muscles typically has a smaller density of receptors and so one finger may not stimulate increased muscle activity.

A variation, the palpation/squeeze, differs from basic palpation in that it uses one to four fingers and the thumb in a pincer-like or squeezing motion to provide an even greater amount of stimulation (see Figure 3.5). Moderate pressure is generally applied with the palpation/squeeze method. (Basic palpation and the squeeze variation are useful techniques when you want the exerciser to remember "phantom fingers." We'll discuss this concept later in this chapter.)

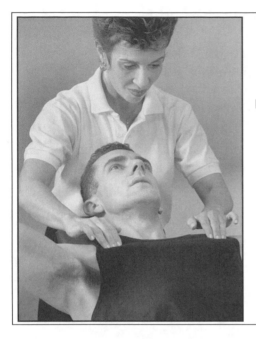

■ *3.4 One to three fingers are used for the basic palpation.*

■ *3.5 One to four fingers and the thumb are used in the squeeze variation.*

Walking

Walking the fingers along a muscle is used primarily to direct the movement. It provides detailed information to the exerciser about the direction of the contraction. As you did in stroking, walk your fingers along the pull of the muscle (Figure 3.6). With a concentric contraction this means walking your fingers from the distal insertion up to the top of the contraction. With an eccentric contraction, walking proceeds downward from the proximal insertion to the point of full extension. When walking with the fingers, use only moderate pressure against the skin.

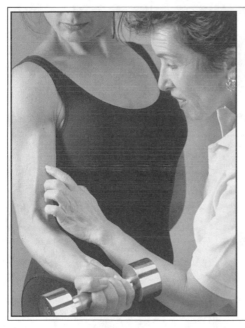

■ *3.6* *Position of the fingers using the walking technique. The trainer should walk the fingers in the direction of the muscle fibers.*

As the fingers contact the skin, you provide the exerciser with sensory feedback about which part of the muscle to next contract. Timing is important. You will want to walk along the muscle at a slow, smooth, and deliberate tempo so that each part of the muscle contracts in an orderly fashion. Although this technique can be used with all muscles, to use it properly you must clearly understand the architecture and line of pull in each muscle.

I sometimes describe the direction of the muscle fibers to my exerciser, but it is not always necessary to do so. Muscle fibers are organized into three different orientations: parallel, pennate, and fan-shaped. However, the techniques I am sharing with you really deal with running your fingers from muscle origin to insertion. In other words, these touch techniques are designed to run in line with the overall direction of the muscle pull, not necessarily in line with the fiber orientation of the muscle.

Once you are familiar with the architecture of a muscle you may want to outline the entire muscle on your exerciser's body using your finger, a skin pencil, or some other type of erasable marker as shown in Figure 3.7a. This is especially helpful when you first begin to work with someone. If you have an entire muscle outlined on the skin and you know in which direction the muscle fibers run, you can begin to use the walking method. This method is not only an effective learning tool but is also fun for both you and your exerciser.

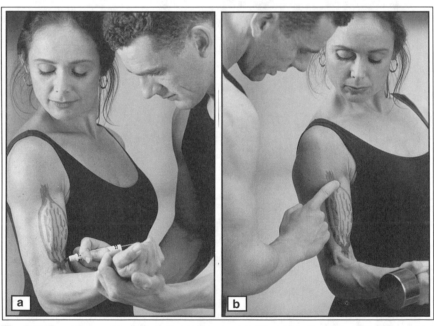

■ *3.7 By using a skin pencil, the trainer can outline the direction of the fibers in a muscle. This will help both the trainer and the exerciser understand the direction the muscle should be contracting (a). Once the muscle has been drawn, the trainer can point out to the exerciser where the proximal and distal insertions are as well as the direction of the overall muscle pull (b).*

Cupping

Use cupping (Figure 3.8) with small muscle groups that, when shortened, become rounded. These groups include the biceps brachii, pectoralis major, and deltoids. By cupping your hand over the muscle you provide a goal or target for your exerciser. This is accomplished by cupping your open hand slightly and asking your exerciser to contract the muscle to fill the cup of your hand. The object is for the exerciser to shorten the muscle maximally. If there is a noticeable filling of the cup, it's likely that the muscle is contracting with maximal tension. To provide a more challenging goal for your exerciser, adjust the shape of your hand to form an increasingly deeper cup.

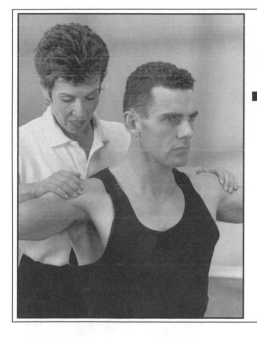

■ *3.8 Using the cupping technique provides a goal for your exerciser—encourage him to fill the cup.*

Knife-Edge

The knife-edge is probably the least used of all the hand methods. By placing the outer edge of your hand between two muscles along his longitudinal axis (see Figure 3.9), you can give your exerciser feedback about the shape and boundary of a specific muscle. The knife-edge is used most often with the inner aspect of the pectorals and the outer aspect of the quadriceps. Essentially, you are providing your exerciser with an outline of his or her muscle. Like cupping, the knife-edge is generally used to provide your exerciser with a goal or a target. However, you can also use it to stimulate the vastus lateralis or the long head of the bicep by moving the edge of your hand upward along the full length of the muscle. This method is most often used during the actual muscle contraction but also occasionally prior to the contraction.

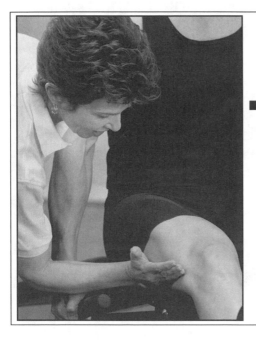

■ *3.9 Use the knife-edge technique to define the shape and boundary of the muscle.*

Phantom Fingers: How to Make a Lasting Impression on the Muscle

But O, for the touch of a vanished hand,
And the sound of a voice that is still.
Alfred, Lord Tennyson

When you have withdrawn your touch and your exerciser remembers where the touch was and how it felt, he is perceiving "phantom fingers." Your exerciser feels as though the fingers are there when in fact they are not. This is one of my favorite techniques. It is very effective and is specific to power, speed, and skill training.

Recall that the two physiological responses to using STT are facilitation of the muscle contraction and feedback to your exerciser about where the contraction should be occurring. Although the absence of touch means that there can be no facilitation, there can still be a lasting effect of a touch persisting in memory. There are two explanations for this phenomenon.

First, some of the receptors in the skin are slow to adapt—that is, when the touch is removed the receptors are slow to adjust to not having the fingers still there. The neural impulses from the receptors continue to be sent to the brain, so it actually feels as if the fingers are still there.

The second explanation is that the feeling of the touch remains in working memory for about 20 to 30 seconds. This works the same way as when you look at a number in the telephone book, remembering the number for a few seconds as you dial, and then forget it a few seconds later. Sensations can remain vivid for a short time, so the phantom fingers are remembered even after the touch is discontinued.

Apply the phantom fingers technique just before the execution of a movement by having your exerciser focus his or her attention on the touch while you use either basic palpation or the squeeze variation with a slightly more rapid and firm touch. While you are touching the skin over the muscle, tell the exerciser to focus on your touch and to vividly recall the touch at the appropriate time while executing the desired movement. Remind your exerciser to think of the phantom fingers and to contract or focus on using the muscle at that particular location. Once this has been done a few times, your exerciser will become comfortable with this technique and will use it more effectively. She or he may even be able to store it in long-term memory so that it is available for recall at any time.

The phantom fingers method is used to focus and hold your exerciser's concentration on a specific area at a specific time during a sequence of moves. For example, to execute complicated movements, such as a power clean or a backhand stroke in tennis, it is vital that your exerciser contract his muscles in the correct sequence. Exercisers often fail to focus on a specific muscle group or fail to do so in time to successfully complete the movement. Self-palpation or palpation by you immediately before the event will not only identify the exact location of the specific muscles but also aid in their timely contraction. Once the exerciser can recall the areas touched, the appropriate timing for the sequence of contractions can be acquired with proper coaching, practice, and feedback.

Who Should Be Touched?

This section should probably be called Who Should *Not* Be Touched. Although STT works with most people, there will be some who will not benefit from its use. For instance, the technique does not work well with people who become defensive when touched. The best way to determine if someone is inhibited by touch is to ask. We recommend that prior to using STT you ask your exercisers whether they have any hesitancy about being touched. You cannot assume that their answers will always be honest, so try to be sensitive to their responses to touch as you decide whether the use of touch training is appropriate.

Touching On Ethics

We strongly recommend that you develop a trusting professional relationship with your exerciser prior to using STT. You need to be especially careful when using the technique with members of the opposite gender. Of course, you must obtain your exerciser's consent before you touch him or her. But beyond that, we strongly urge that you and your exerciser discuss what is acceptable and what is not. Your exercisers should also be advised that they can withdraw their consent at any time if they become uncomfortable with the technique.

Use caution when using STT with people you know or suspect have been victims of sexual abuse. Also, be aware that every state has different laws regarding contact with minors. Training by touch requires the trainer to conform to the same professional and ethical standards as any other health care professional. You'll need to use good judgment in each situation.

Is This Method for You?

How do *you* feel about being touched? Are you relaxed and comfortable? Or does such contact make you tense? To use STT successfully, you must be clear about how you feel about someone touching you in an exercise setting. Only then can you be sensitive to the fears and anxieties of others. Think too about how comfortable you are with touching others. If you feel awkward at first, don't be discouraged. With practice, touching becomes automatic and is quite natural.

What's Your Learning Preference?

Of the five sensory systems, do you know which your client relies on primarily to receive information from the environment? This knowledge may affect the success you have using STT with any given exerciser.

Each of us learns differently. Some of us prefer verbal instruction or to listen to a cassette tape; others would rather watch a videotape or a live demonstration. Some prefer to read; others want to touch and be touched. The scientific discipline *psycholinguistics* has evolved to explore how the knowledge of one's preferential sensory mode influences learning and interpersonal communications. Of course, knowing the exerciser's preferred learning style helps you to design an individualized exercise program.

When using STT, trainers often use their own preferred style rather than the preferred style of their exercisers. This is a common error that should be avoided to ensure good communication between exerciser and trainer. But the ability to switch to the exerciser's preferred mode requires practice. First, you need to determine whether your exerciser prefers to learn through reading, listening to instructions, visual demonstration, hands-on techniques, or through trial and error. Most people respond best to a combination of modes. Adding STT to any one preferred style or combination of preferred styles usually enhances learning and performance.

Ask your exercisers which learning mode they prefer. If they cannot answer, then quiz them on the kinds of activities they prefer among reading, watching, listening, and doing. Most people are aware of their preference, and this information should be sufficient for you to determine which style to emphasize.

If your exerciser has a strong kinesthetic sense, then STT will allow him to learn new exercises rapidly. During rest intervals, have the exerciser touch *your* muscles at the critical locations as you perform the exercise. He should then try to duplicate the movement. This is a teaching technique I use frequently to accelerate learning.

When Should You Touch?

You must determine at the onset of the workout session whether STT should be used at all. There are two reasons not to use STT. First, although most exercisers who suffer from stress or anxiety prefer to work hard, others do not wish to be pushed. In the latter case, STT should not be used. Second, exercisers who show signs of mental or physical fatigue are not likely to respond positively to touch. In such cases, you should either complete the workout without using STT, or you should terminate the workout.

Once you have learned to use STT, you can use touch methods either before your exerciser begins or while the muscle is contracting. Based on what we have discussed so far, it is apparent that any touch before the onset of exercise will not facilitate the strength of the contraction, but it can provide sensory feedback about which muscle or area of a muscle should be contracted.

The information that you can provide to your exerciser prior to the exercise includes the direction the contraction should follow, the boundaries of each of the contracting muscles, and the exact sequence of the desired contractions (use phantom fingers when appropriate).

We believe that administering a touch during the exercise not only helps exercisers refocus if they have lost their concentration, but it also initiates a reflex that results in a stronger contraction. Doing this is particularly useful because it recruits additional motor units throughout the muscle during a contraction and at the onset of fatigue.

How Often Should You Touch?

In the early stages of learning, administer touch during each repetition of a given set so that neural connections between the voluntary muscle contraction and the reflexive muscle contraction can be established in your exerciser's memory. Once he or she has established a consistent and mechanically correct movement, you will not need to touch the muscle during every contraction. At this point, intermittent and random touching is recommended.

If you always touch at the same time, the exerciser will come to expect it, which could eliminate the advantage of using STT. This principle is well known among psychologists. For example, after years of study behavioral psychologist B.F. Skinner found that at the early stages of learning constant feedback leads to rapid improvement in performance; once the desired behavior has been learned occasional feedback is more effective.

There are five basic reasons to use STT:

1. To evaluate for muscle tension and muscle imbalances
2. To facilitate a muscle contraction
3. To provide feedback to the exerciser
4. To help focus attention on the muscle
5. To encourage muscle relaxation

You should use STT as frequently as necessary to accomplish these goals. Once they have been achieved, you should decrease the frequency to an occasional touch, or even refrain from touching. No absolute rules govern the frequency of touch. Ultimately, the decision to decrease the frequency depends on the needs of the exerciser.

How Hard Should You Touch?

The ambiguity of such words as "hard" and "soft" makes it difficult to describe how much pressure you should apply when touching. To solve this problem, we have developed a scale that uses analogies to describe the amount of pressure you should use in various situations. The scale is exerciser specific: Each individual's sensations determine his or her own scale.

As you can see in Figure 3.10, the intensity scale ranges from 1 to 5. For clarity, we'll define the pressure at levels 1 and 5 so that you can instruct your exercisers on what they would feel at these intensities.

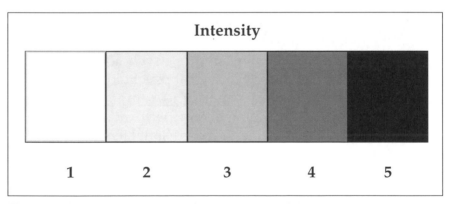

■ *3.10 The intensity of the touch in STT ranges from 1-5, with 1 representing the lightest touch and 5 representing the touch with the most pressure. The intensities of 1 and 5 are never used.*

At level 1, pressure is very light—almost like a tickle or a fly landing on your skin. This level represents the low end of the range of intensities and is never used. Such a light touch typically elicits fear, annoyance, or arousal. For some, the touch feels sexual. All of these responses are inappropriate for STT.

Level 5 is at the upper end of the range of intensities and is defined as a painful touch that leads to extreme discomfort. Such a touch serves no purpose in STT.

To establish a scale for each of your exercisers, use the following procedures:

1. Touch the underside of your exerciser's forearm very lightly. While touching, instruct the exerciser to indicate when the touch feels like a tickle. This touch represents level 1 on the scale of intensity (see Figure 3.11).

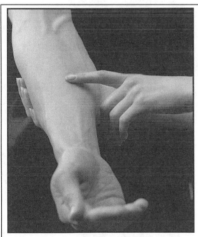

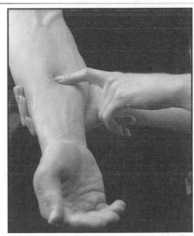

■ *3.11 Resting the exerciser's forearm on your hand, have him identify intensity 1. It is never used with STT.*

■ *3.12 Resting the exerciser's forearm on your hand, have him identify intensity 5. It causes pain and is never used with STT.*

2. Next, increase the pressure gradually until your exerciser indicates feelings of pain. This amount of pressure represents level 5 (Figure 3.12). It is *very* important to remember generally how much pressure you applied at levels 1 and 5. Pain thresholds differ for each individual.

Once you have established these two endpoints, you can determine the middle three levels: 2, 3, and 4. These are the three intensities you will use with STT for this exerciser.

3. **Exert the amount of pressure corresponding to level 1.** As you begin to press harder, ask your exerciser to indicate the midpoint between 1 and 5 (see Figure 3.13). He should say "3" at this midpoint. Repeat this procedure until you have a good understanding of how much pressure to exert.

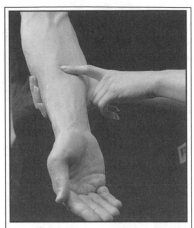

■ *3.13 Pressure identified by the exerciser as halfway between intensities 1 and 5 is considered to be intensity 3, or **moderate** pressure.*

4. **After establishing levels 1, 3, and 5, use the same procedure to determine levels 2 and 4.** Your exerciser should indicate the pressure halfway between 1 and 3 and then between 3 and 5 (see Figures 3.14 and 3.15). Repeat the process until you can consistently exert pressures of intensities 2, 3, and 4. Intensity level 2 is considered light, 3 moderate, and 4 firm.

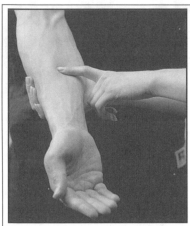

■ *3.14 Pressure identified by the exerciser as the midpoint between intensities 1 and 3 is designated 2, or **light** pressure.*

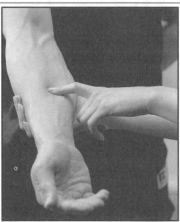

■ *3.15 Have your exerciser indicate the pressure halfway between 3 and 5 to determine intensity 4, or **firm** pressure.*

In Table 3.2 we have provided you with a simple guide that describes the intensities that should be used with each hand technique.

Table 3.2 Intensity Scale			
Method	**Intensity***		
	Light Intensity 2	**Moderate Intensity 3**	**Firm Intensity 4**
Maintained touch	▓		
Stroking		▓	▓
Palpation/squeeze	▓	▓	
Walking	▓	▓	
Cupping	▓	▓	
Knife-edge	▓	▓	
Phantom fingers		▓	▓
Evaluation	▓		
Stimulation		▓	▓
Relaxation	▓		
Giving direction to contraction	▓	▓	▓ **
Focusing attention	▓	▓	▓ **
Delaying muscle fatigue		▓	▓

*Although there are three categories of intensity, please note that intensity is on a continuum. Within each category there is a range of intensities.
**Intensity 4 should be used with phantom fingers only

How Fast Should You Touch?

The speed at which you touch also affects the success of STT. By "speed," we mean how fast you move your hand when touching. To help you remember the approximate speeds at which to move your hands in different situations, we will suggest three metaphors. Use these as guides until you are comfortable with the technique. Speed, like intensity and hand positions, will become second nature when you are working with your exerciser.

Use STT at one of three speeds: slow, medium, or rapid. A slow movement is like using your hand to carefully trace a detailed picture. Medium speed is like petting a cat. Rapid speed is like wiping away a spot on your clothing.

Follow three rules to determine how fast to move in different situations:

• **Rule #1** involves the amount of experience your exerciser has with a particular exercise. With experienced exercisers, you may move fast. With inexperienced exercisers, move more slowly. A beginner likely has not developed the necessary motor control and coordination to perform the exercise correctly. By moving slowly you will decrease the number of mistakes made.

• **Rule #2** is determined by the intensity of the workout. Generally, as intensity increases, so should the speed of your touch. Try to maintain the same tempo or rhythm during the entire set.

• **Rule #3** is determined by the goal of the specific exercise—whether you are training for power or for endurance. If your exerciser is performing muscle contractions at high speed (power), then your touch should be administered rapidly before the beginning of the exercise (phantom fingers technique). Of course, you would not want to try and touch a muscle during a ballistic muscle contraction, such as during power lifting. In contrast, if your exerciser is completing an endurance workout in which the speed of the contraction is relatively slow, the speed of your touch should also be slower.

In summary, use three speeds: slow, medium, and rapid. The speed most appropriate in a specific situation is determined by the experience of your exerciser with the exercise, the overall intensity of the workout, and the speed of the contraction.

Four More Questions

Before we continue with step-by-step instructions and guidelines for the practical use of STT, let's pause to consider four important questions.

- How can STT be used to provide biofeedback?
- Can you do *too much* touching when using the touch method?
- How can you use touch to detect the onset of muscle fatigue?
- What is the difference between touching for stimulation and touching for relaxation?

We will discuss each of these questions separately in the sections that follow.

How Can STT Be Used to Provide Biofeedback?

STT is a form of *biofeedback*, or biological feedback—a technique people use to control their internal processes. For example, a person who normally becomes anxious in stressful situations and feels the heart beating faster can learn to reduce the stress by monitoring and eventually controlling the heart rate. This can be done by displaying the person's heart rate on a screen and asking her to attempt to reduce the rate through conscious control. This way the patient receives feedback (the visual display) about a biological process (the heart rate) that she or he would otherwise be unable to recognize. Biofeedback can be used to monitor a variety of other physiological responses, including contraction of individual muscle fibers, muscle tension, brain activity, and breathing. Biofeedback allows people to gain control over their bodies by using their minds. The skills developed through biofeedback can be used at any time.

In our touch training system, the electronic device or feedback machine is replaced with a human partner responsible for monitoring muscle activity with the hand and communicating with the exerciser verbally. By touching a muscle during an exercise, a trainer can assure that the exerciser is contracting the correct muscle. As we have said, we know that people often contract incorrect muscles during exercise because they can't tell they are doing so. Hence, the information the trainer provides to the client is valuable. Many exercises allow you to use this method on yourself.

In addition to monitoring which muscle is contracting, you can also monitor both the amount and the source of tension in the muscle. Palpating the skin covering the muscle enables you to determine which part needs to be further contracted. Placing your hand on that location allows your exerciser to focus on contracting that area of the muscle. For example, if your exerciser tires while performing a set of biceps curls, a touch to the skin over the biceps reminds him or her to continue producing tension in that muscle.

John Basmajian, a muscle physiologist and a pioneer in the use of biofeedback to control muscle contraction, found that many people can consciously contract and relax a single group of muscle fibers if they receive biofeedback about how much tension those muscle fibers are producing. Using sophisticated equipment, Basmajian was able to monitor which muscle fibers within a whole muscle were contracting and which were not. He then told his experimental subjects which part of the muscle was not contracting. With this information, his subjects were able to selectively contract individual motor units.

While touching an entire muscle or even a small part of it, it is possible for a trainer to tell exercisers how much tension they are creating. Exercisers are then able to contract a few selected muscle fibers within a whole muscle. Although Basmajian's experiments used equipment to measure muscle activity precisely, it is my experience that with a little practice you can detect even small changes in muscle tension simply by feeling the muscle.

STT provides information to your exercisers that they could not obtain on their own. They can use this information to control the muscle more efficiently. Through repeated STT, your exercisers learn which muscle to contract during an exercise; this information is then stored in long-term memory. For example, an exerciser may have developed the habit of performing a latissimus pull-down by first contracting the biceps and only later using the latissimus to complete the movement. STT can direct your exerciser's attention toward avoiding the primary use of the biceps and learning how to initiate the exercise using the latissimus. By repeatedly using STT, your exerciser learns to do the exercise correctly.

Can STT Be Overused?

Yes, STT is an effective technique for improving muscle strength and function, but it is possible to do too much. By "too much," we mean going beyond just touching. If you *move* your exerciser's limbs during the exercise, you can actually inhibit the learning of correct muscle contraction patterns. When using STT, you should touch the skin without moving the limb.

Many trainers and coaches advocate manually moving a person's limb(s) when teaching a new movement. In his recent text, *Motor Learning and Performance*, Richard Schmidt suggests that this is not an effective teaching strategy and that moving the limb actually *decreases* the amount of feedback your exerciser receives. Much of the information that the brain receives during a muscle contraction comes from the motor centers of the brain where the neural impulses to the muscle are initiated. Scientists call this information *efference copy*. When the neural commands are sent to the muscle to contract, a copy of the same neural commands travel to the sensory centers in the brain. When someone moves your arm for you, you are not actually contracting the muscle yourself, so there is no efferent copy. This deprives your brain of valuable information about a movement. Therefore, it is important that you allow your exerciser to at least initiate the movement.

With STT, you need only touch the muscle while it is contracting. STT is *not* manual movement—it is a method for facilitating the contraction of a muscle.

How Can Touch Be Used to Detect the Onset of Muscle Fatigue?

Most exercisers know when their muscles are tiring. But you may be surprised to learn that a trainer can often detect a loss of tension in the muscle even before the exerciser feels weakness. I can best describe this tension loss as a subtle faltering in the strength of the contraction in a particular area of the muscle. It feels as if the tension slightly fades under your fingertips. I cannot always detect these small changes in tension, but when I do, I can frequently "save" the muscle for two or three more repetitions by using palpation/squeeze or stroking. These hand techniques should be applied at a moderate to firm intensity at a medium to rapid speed. I generally direct my touch to the full length of the muscle on the lateral and medial sides, which are often underutilized and from where we believe additional motor units can be recruited. At the same time, it is important to give your exercisers feedback and encourage them to produce more tension in the muscle.

Your challenge is to detect weakness before total fatigue occurs. It doesn't matter who recognizes the weakness first, you or your exercisers, so don't hesitate to ask them how many repetitions they think they have left.

Relaxation Versus Stimulation: How Does the Touch Differ?

You may use STT either to stimulate the contraction of a muscle or to help a muscle relax. The difference is in the speed and intensity of your touch and in your verbal instructions.

You may wonder why you would ever want to relax a muscle during an exercise. If you recall, we discussed earlier the optimal pattern of muscle contraction to produce maximum strength. To maximize the amount of force a target muscle can produce, it is necessary to relax the antagonistic muscle or group of muscles. It is easy to understand the reason for this. Consider that there are two muscle groups that flex and extend the lower arm around the elbow—the biceps brachii and the triceps brachii. Imagine that both are contracting maximally at the same time. Which way do you think the lower arm will move? Try it—you'll find it won't move at all. So, to flex the elbow with maximal strength (i.e., contract the biceps), the triceps should produce minimal force, if any. For the most part, if the triceps contract, they prevent the biceps from flexing the elbow maximally.

Be careful not to touch antagonist muscles at the same time that you are attempting to stimulate a contraction in the target muscle. For a maximal contraction of the target muscle, you must first relax the antagonist muscles. Actually, *all* inappropriately tensed muscles that are impeding the movement should be relaxed, even if they are not antagonists. A properly administered touch can accomplish this. We'll call this specific touch technique the *touch-to-relax* technique.

You'll use the touch-to-relax technique in two situations. The first is when inappropriate tension is generated in a muscle. An example would be tension in the upper trapezius muscle during a standing biceps curl. I recently demonstrated my touch technique to a friend training a bodybuilder. During biceps curls, the exerciser was obviously "trapping" his way through every repetition.

"I've tried everything to get those shoulders down and relax the traps," my friend said. "I've instructed and explained. I've ordered and poked. But nothing works. If he drops them for one rep, they go right back up on the next."

I offered to try to help. First, I asked the exerciser if he could relax his trapezius and let his shoulders drop. He answered with some annoyance, "They are relaxed." But I could see they were not. Next, I stood behind him and placed my hands on either side of his neck, resting them lightly on the upper trapezius. I then asked him to focus on my touch for a moment and to relax the muscles underneath my hands. His shoulders dropped significantly! I could feel the upper trapezius muscles soften, almost as if they were melting under my hands. I removed my hands as he continued his repetitions, but every third rep or so, I touched him lightly on the trapezius. Leaving my hands stationary over the muscle, I used a light maintained touch with a very slight back-and-forth motion (about 2 seconds). As I did this, I instructed him to stay relaxed. To verify that the tension was now redirected to his biceps, I placed my hands over both biceps to feel for renewed tension.

My trainer friend had the right idea. She had tried to touch the trapezius to identify the point of tension for the exerciser, but her touch was too prodding and invasive. The repeated pushing and prodding may have stimulated the muscle to remain tense even while she tried to encourage him to relax. By my simply reducing the intensity and speed of the touch, the muscle had a chance to respond appropriately.

The second use of touch to relax a muscle is during stretching. Touch can be used in the "relax" phase of a PNF stretch or during a static stretch when the muscle feels as if it will no longer respond to a sustained stretch. As in the previous example, you simply place your hand in a maintained touch on the belly of the muscle (or wherever you feel particular tightness). Use a light-to-moderate touch and encourage your exerciser to focus on the point you are touching and to think about releasing the muscle in the area of your touch. I have found this an extremely effective technique to move deeper into and maximize any stretch.

As with all stretching techniques, best results are achieved when your exerciser exhales while attempting to move deeper into the stretch. Try to reduce the intensity of your voice as you talk your exerciser through the stretches. One of the rewards of this technique is to witness an exerciser's satisfaction with the sensation of being able to release and relax deeper into the stretch. One note: This technique in no way obviates trainer-assisted stretches. There is no push, no pull, and no deep massaging or deep stroking to encourage a muscle to relax. Think of the STT touch-to-relax technique as an adjunct to the trainer-assisted maximal stretch.

Summary

STT employs seven basic methods of touch: maintained touch, stroking, palpation/squeeze, walking, cupping, and knife-edge. Maintained touch is the primary method to use for evaluation. Cupping, stroking, walking, and/or palpation/squeeze are the methods most often used to stimulate the muscle. Stroking, maintained touch, and basic palpation are the methods most often employed for relaxation. A separate form of palpation, phantom fingers, is specific to power, speed, and skill training. To determine whether an exerciser will benefit from STT a trainer should consider the exerciser's personal inhibitions and learning preferences.

We've discussed intensity of touch, speed of touch, and frequency of touch. The intensity of touch is represented on an exerciser-specific scale of 1 to 5. Touch to facilitate a contraction is generally of moderate intensity, whereas touch-to-relax requires a light-to-moderate intensity. Phantom fingers needs a firm touch. Accompany all three methods with verbal instructions. The speed of touch is determined by the experience of the exerciser, the intensity of the workout, and the speed of the contraction. STT should be used frequently in the early stages of training and less frequently when the movement has been learned.

STT is an effective method of biofeedback. The trainer can determine by touch if the exerciser is contracting the correct muscle and which part of the muscle needs to be further contracted. This information is then communicated to the exerciser, enabling him or her to contract selected muscle fibers as needed. However, STT requires that the exerciser initiate the exercise himself.

Similarly, STT can help detect the onset of muscle fatigue, recognized by subtle changes in muscle tension. If fatigue is discovered in time, it is often possible to recruit additional motor units to help delay total muscle fatigue. The hand techniques employed for this purpose are palpation/squeeze or stroking. The intensity of touch to delay the effects of muscle fatigue is moderate to firm and the speed medium to rapid.

IT'S TIME TO TRAIN

How to Use STT: Part II

> It is best to do things systematically,
> since we are only human, and
> disorder is our worst enemy.
>
> Hesiod (Eighth century B.C.)

In this second half of our introduction to the STT system, you will learn about the four components of the exercise session. We believe that if you use these techniques step-by-step, you will avoid confusion and frustration for both yourself and your exercisers. We suggest that you follow this four-step procedure when using STT for the first time.

Step 1: **Warm up and observation**

Step 2: **Explanation**

Step 3: **Evaluation**

Step 4: **Instruction and feedback**

You should use all four steps when working with a beginner, but you'll need only steps 1, 3, and 4 with experienced STT users. In this chapter we will elaborate on these procedures and provide helpful hints to improve your understanding of and ability to use STT.

Step 1: Warm Up and Observation

As in any exercise session, the first step is the warm-up. Warming up involves light aerobic activities and stretches that prepare the body for the upcoming workout. A warm-up is particularly important when using STT because it is better to touch the muscle after increased blood flow has been directed to the target muscle. The muscle becomes more sensitive to touch with increased blood flow. We'll presume that readers of this book have taught proper warm-up and stretching exercises, so we'll not discuss them here.

During the first few minutes of the workout session, have your exerciser perform the exercise at low intensity without any instruction or discussion of the STT system. This allows you to observe your exerciser's technique and determine whether the correct muscles are being used. You are not touching here but only watching. If the exerciser is a beginner, anticipate several problems (of course, this is sometimes true with experienced exercisers as well), but try to avoid critical comments and instead provide encouragement and support.

Step 2: Explanation

At this stage, introduce the STT system to your exercisers. Offer a brief explanation of STT, what it is designed to accomplish, and its potential benefits. Ask the exercisers for permission to touch them during the exercise session and inform them of their right to deny or withdraw permission at any time. It is important to discuss what is and what is not acceptable touching, especially if you and an exerciser are of opposite genders.

Remember to tell exercisers exactly where you are about to touch before doing so. We recommend you develop your own explanation and style. However, keep the explanation simple because too much information can cause confusion. You might say something like this:

> I'd like to try using a new training technique that involves touching the muscle you should be contracting during an exercise. This will improve your concentration and help you to focus on the muscle. It might increase the strength of your muscle contractions by stimulating your central nervous system, which will allow better communication between your brain and your muscles. I'll use this technique along with our regular training program because it enhances other training methods. I won't need to actually touch your skin because it is just as effective over light clothing. But I need your consent before I start. You can change your mind at any time if you feel uncomfortable, or for any other reason. I won't be offended. We need to decide in advance what you feel is comfortable and appropriate because you should be completely at ease during the exercise session. With your permission, I may want to outline a particular muscle on your body with my index finger or with a skin pencil so that you will know exactly where to direct your focus. During the exercises I may also feel your muscles to evaluate whether they are contracting maximally. If they are not, I'll tell you what to do to make the necessary adjustments.

After explaining our touch training technique, establish the exerciser's scale of pressure (refer to chapter 3). Then present the exercise and describe its purpose, the muscles that should be involved, and their function. Next, have your exerciser contract the target muscle while you touch or palpate the origin, insertion, and belly of the muscle. Then outline the direction of the muscle pull. With a beginner or an exerciser in need of a more detailed anatomical explanation, you may want to use the skin pencil or your index finger to outline the location and shape of the muscle and its attachments. Touching the skin over the muscle will help your exerciser develop a mental picture of his muscle. Don't worry if you sometimes miss the exact location of the insertion or origin of the muscle. This may be difficult for even a registered physical therapist or a doctor to instantly locate every time. Determine the general length and width of the muscle you are working.

Step 3: Evaluation

With accurate hands-on evaluation techniques, you can achieve two important objectives. First, you can determine if an exerciser is using the correct muscles to perform a given exercise. People commonly attempt to lift more weight than they are capable of and consequently "cheat" by using muscles not intended to be exercised. This typically causes muscle imbalances that may lead to injuries. There are two types of muscle imbalances: overinvolvement of synergistic muscles and bilateral asymmetry. For example, when your exerciser performs chest flys, you can evaluate whether he is relying on his shoulders, back, biceps, or forearms more than the pectorals (see Figure 4.1). You can also use STT to pick up subtle indications of asymmetric muscle tension in the left and right pectorals (see Figure 4.2). Both of these imbalances lead to improper muscle development. However, once they are recognized you can redirect the movement and explain the correct exercise technique. As a result, your exerciser develops stronger pectorals by using the appropriate target muscle.

Second, you can provide instant feedback to your exerciser. Research on motor skill acquisition has confirmed that immediate and precise feedback is necessary to ensure rapid improvement in skill performance. If you can provide your exerciser with instant feedback about the outcome of each repetition, he will be able to make immediate adjustments that lead to more rapid strength gains.

Evaluation occurs both before and during a contraction. It provides the information you need for making corrections in

■ **4.1.** *Use touch to evaluate for overinvolvement of synergist muscles, such as the deltoids during chest flys.*

■ **4.2.** *Use touch to evaluate for bilateral symmetry during exercises, such as chest flys.*

the pattern of muscle contraction. Evaluation allows you to determine if the contraction is maximal and if the entire muscle is being used. When we use the term "evaluation," we are referring to *hands-on* assessment. What we cannot sense visually, we can often feel through our tactile sense. Throughout the exercise session, you should occasionally evaluate the tension in each of the muscles or muscle groups being worked. You should evaluate the tension just prior to a contraction to ensure that your exerciser is not using inappropriate muscles. We'll cover this point in greater detail in chapter 5.

Step 4: Instruction and Feedback

Instruction and feedback come immediately after the hands-on evaluation, often occurring in the same set of repetitions. For example, in a set of 12 repetitions, you may evaluate during repetitions 1 through 5 and then instruct and give feedback during the rest of the set. This allows you to furnish the exerciser with immediate feedback and the necessary verbal and tactile instructions to correct or adjust the movement. As soon as you feel the exerciser responding to your instructions and your touch, give immediate verbal feedback confirming the effort. This way your exerciser knows that the corrections were accurate and had immediate positive results.

All exercisers should be in proper body alignment. Have yours begin the exercise slowly while you use the stroking method to guide the direction of the contraction. Have the exerciser complete several repetitions while you provide verbal feedback. You might also try to get some feedback by saying at the end of the set, "Show me specifically where you felt the exercise working." This answer will help you determine whether the desired effect is being produced within the target muscle. If the answer is something like, "I didn't feel it at all" or "somewhere around here" (pointing to a nonspecific area), this generally indicates a lack of focus. Do not underestimate the value of your exerciser's feedback, as it is an important factor in achieving proper results. Your exerciser's response will often dictate your next move.

Next, use stroking, palpating, or cupping to provide stimulation, focus, and feedback. For example, if you determine during the exercise that a portion of the muscle is not fully contracting, simply tell the exerciser where he should create more muscle tension while you palpate that specific area. The touch directs your exerciser's attention to the target muscle. Remember that one of the simplest and most effective aspects of STT is that it focuses attention. It helps the exerciser to concentrate on the task at hand and learn to perform the movement correctly.

Finally, touch intermittently as your exerciser completes the regular program. Depending on your goal for the particular workout session, you may want to facilitate the contraction as the muscle fatigues. You should also continue to periodically evaluate and make corrections while encouraging the exerciser to relax any muscles producing unwanted tension (refer to chapter 3, Relaxation Versus Stimulation).

The trainer can feel through touch when a muscle is truly fatigued, and at that point the exercise should end. So, touch is not only to encourage a muscle to continue and delay fatigue, it is also used to indicate that a muscle is no longer working effectively. If the synergist muscles are carrying on the movement, it is time to end the exercise.

HELPFUL HINTS

Here are some additional hints that may help you use the touch technique more effectively.

- Never use STT during power lifts (except for phantom fingers).
- Never touch casually. Each touch should have a distinct purpose. Your touch message should be clear and uncomplicated.
- Maintain your own proper body mechanics to avoid injury to yourself.

- Try to keep your hands clean and oil-free to increase your tactile sensitivity.

- You should be sensitive to the exerciser's pain threshold and stresses. Do not push beyond his or her tolerance with comments like "Come on, you can do it." It is your responsibility to prevent injury.

- Try to be consistent with cues and terminology. Concise verbal and touch cuing is important to a coordinated movement.

- Do not overlook the importance of rhythm. Your voice and rhythm of touch should be consistent with the desired tempo of the workout and the natural body rhythm of your exerciser.

- Adapt your tone of voice. When you want to relax or stretch the muscle, soften your voice. When you want a more forceful contraction, speak in a more energetic tone.

- Do not engage in casual small talk with your exerciser while touching. Any comments should be direct and informational, relating to the exercise technique or performance.

- When touching with two hands, remove one hand at a time. A sudden cessation of touch is itself a stimulus.

- Position the exerciser into the correct body alignment by touching the side to which you want him or her to move, lift, or contract (see Figure 4.3).

- Don't rush the touch! Give your exerciser's mind and body time to respond to the stimulus.

- When touching your exerciser, try to avoid unnecessary eye contact.

- Never touch your exerciser's face.

- For a "clean read" of muscle activity, close your eyes as you are touching the muscle.

- When using STT for any purpose other than evaluation, be sure to tell your exerciser to focus on the muscle being touched.

- Perfect your STT techniques by constantly practicing on your own muscles (see Figure 4.4).

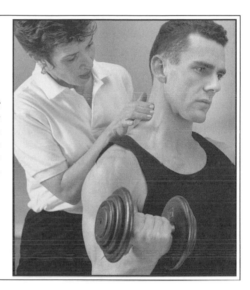

■ **4.3.** *To keep head in correct alignment and eliminate tilting to one side, touch the neck on the side toward which you want it to move and provide accompanying verbal instructions.*

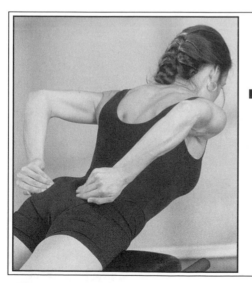

■ **4.4.** *Use the self-touch technique to learn how a muscle should feel when properly relaxing or contracting. Experience how your own mind and muscles respond to touch so that you can better communicate what you want your exerciser to feel.*

Summary

Systematic touch training is a four-step procedure. You first prepare exercisers for their workouts by having them warm up while you observe form and technique. Next, you offer an explanation of the exercise and the muscles to be used when performing it. Third, you conduct a hands-on evaluation of the muscles to determine whether they are being used correctly during the exercise. Finally, be sure to provide instruction, stimulation, focus, and feedback to the exerciser during the exercise.

CHAPTER Five

NOW TRY *YOUR* HAND

To teach is to learn twice over.

Joseph Joubert (1842)

To describe the use of Systematic T.O.U.C.H. Training procedures with all of the muscle groups and various types of equipment currently available would require several chapters and hundreds of pages. Instead, we have divided the major muscle groups into three general categories (see Table 5.1) and will explain how to use STT when exercising the muscles in each one.

Because each muscle group is different with respect to size, shape, and function, the application of STT will vary depending on the muscle type. Take the cupping method, for example. This method is effective when working with small, round muscles, such as the biceps or triceps, but it is not useful with the latissimus because the muscle is large and flat and there is no rounding of the muscle during contraction.

We have chosen to use as our examples the biceps brachii (small and round), the quadriceps (large and round), and the latissimus dorsi (large and flat). Due to popular demand, we

Table 5.1

List of Selected Muscles by Category of Size and Shape

Category	Characteristic	Muscles
I	Small size Round shape	Biceps brachii Triceps brachii Deltoids Trapezius Gastrocnemius
II	Large size Round shape	Pectoralis major Gluteus maximus Gluteus medius Quadriceps Hamstrings
III	Large size Flat shape	Latissimus dorsi Abdominals

have also included a discussion of the abdominals. The sections that follow are organized according to the four components of the exercise session that we described in chapter 4:

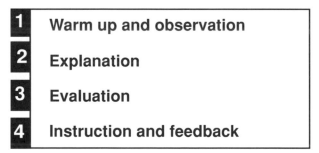

1 Warm up and observation

2 Explanation

3 Evaluation

4 Instruction and feedback

The same procedures can be applied when exercising all of the other muscles in each of the three categories and to all of the possible exercises that can be performed by each muscle. To illustrate this, we have provided in the appendix 23 additional exercises that involve all of the major muscle groups. We strongly recommend that you begin by carefully reading all four examples, as we have added information and useful tips to each example that may apply to all other exercises.

EXAMPLE ONE

MUSCLE TYPE
Biceps Brachii
(small round muscles)

EXERCISE
**Standing Dumbbell
Biceps Curl**

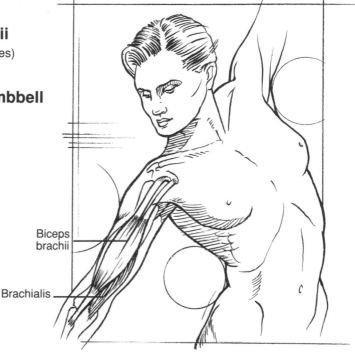

Biceps
brachii

Brachialis

1 | Warm Up and Observation

You can use a light aerobic activity along with lightweight biceps curls to help prepare the muscle for the sets that follow. Do not allow your exerciser to skip the warm-up because she is too anxious to begin the workout. The lightweight warm-up is an excellent opportunity to start your observation of technique and body alignment.

These are some common errors you may detect during visual observation of the standing dumbbell biceps curl.

- Rapid snapping or jerking movements that throw the weight up toward the shoulders
- "Cheating" by moving the shoulder slightly backward and scooping under or rocking to bring the weight up
- Failure to fully extend the arms at the end of each repetition

- Failure to keep the elbows stationary and close to the sides of the body as the weight is raised and lowered
- Gripping the hands too tightly around the dumbbells
- Failure to maintain wrist joints in neutral position
- Failure to *slowly* lower the weight to the starting position before repeating the movement
- Slouching forward or arching back at any point during the exercise
- Failure to move the weight upward toward the shoulder in an arc
- Failure to maximize the concentric contraction

2 Explanation

Most exercisers are familiar with the biceps exercise, but offering simple, detailed information about the muscle piques their interest and helps achieve more effective results from each set. Outline the muscle with your index finger or skin pencil, identify points of origin and insertion and the outside and inside (lateral and medial) boundaries, describe its line of pull, and explain what the muscle is designed to do (see Figure 5.1). These techniques help to reinforce and expand the exerciser's knowledge.

Muscle Description 2

You may wish to offer the following explanation.

Biceps Brachii. The biceps brachii and the brachialis are two major muscles of the upper arm. The biceps is a small, round muscle with two heads that originate above the shoulder joint and inserts below the elbow joint on the radius (i.e., lower arm). The two heads have slightly different functions. The long head, which lies on the outside of the upper arm (stroke the outside edge of the biceps with one finger or use the knife-edge), flexes the elbow and raises the lower arm. The short head (stroke the inside edge of the biceps with one finger or use the knife-edge), located on the inside of the upper arm, supinates (outwardly rotates) the hand and flexes the elbow.

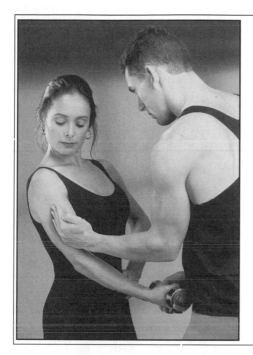

■ **5.1** *While describing how the biceps works, use the knife-edge to outline its lateral boundary.*

Brachialis.   The other muscle that both crosses and flexes the elbow is the brachialis, which lies deep below the biceps. Although both the biceps brachii and the brachialis are elbow flexors, the brachialis is bigger and stronger. The biceps gives the desirable shape to the upper arm, but the brachialis gives it size.

Brachioradialis.   The other muscle that assists in elbow flexion is the brachioradialis, which lies in the forearm. Note that if you are working your biceps, you do not want the brachioradialis to take over and do most of the work.

Fiber Direction.   The biceps consist of muscle fibers that run in the same direction from the shoulder to the elbow. So, when working the biceps, the best line of pull would be a straight line between the shoulder and the elbow.

Movements Involving Biceps Muscles 2

We use the biceps to pick up, pull up, or hold an object. It is particularly important in such movements as chinning and working with gymnastic rings.

3 | Evaluation

It is not always possible to just look at the biceps and determine if they are contracting correctly (i.e., symmetrically and with appropriate tension). It is helpful to also touch the skin over the muscle to feel the action taking place.

During the evaluation and/or the instruction and feedback phases of the biceps exercise you may use some or all of the following methods of touch:

- Maintained touch
- Stroking
- Palpation/squeeze
- Cupping
- Knife-edge
- Walking
- Touch-to-relax
- Phantom fingers

Evaluating Body Alignment 3

See that your exerciser is in the proper stance for a standing dumbbell biceps curl. Correct any gross errors such as a sunken chest or locked knees, but refrain from correcting minor errors such as a head tilt or turn or a chin drop until you feel the biceps working. You will deal with these minor adjustments as necessary during the instruction and feedback phase. You may also want to stand behind the exerciser and place your hands on both biceps in a maintained touch position. Feel for a subtle weight shift backward, which you may detect not only from a slight movement by your exerciser toward you, but also from a subtle reduction in the strength of the contraction. Instruct her to shift her body weight to the balls of her feet while executing the curl.

Evaluating Initiation 3

Using your cupped hands or three or more fingers, touch the biceps just prior to the movement and throughout the first few contractions. Before the first movement of the lower arm, you will want to feel if there is tension in the muscle. If the lower arm or any body part (e.g., shoulder or wrist) moves before the tension is produced in the biceps, then your exerciser is using muscles other than the target muscle to initiate the movement. It is important not to allow the exerciser to continue the exercise until you feel the tension beneath your hands. This process is analogous to driving a car with one foot on the accelerator and the other foot on the brake. As the brake pedal is released, the car moves instantly. If the feet were not on the accelerator and the brake at the same time, a pause would occur between when the foot is lifted off the brake and when the accelerator is depressed. Before moving a limb, tension should be produced in the muscle so that the movement occurs instantly when the exerciser decides to execute it.

Evaluating Bilateral Symmetry 3

As we indicated in chapter 4, you will want to feel for bilateral muscle imbalances. Check to see if the same muscles on both sides of the body are contracting symmetrically (see Figure 5.2). Ask yourself, "Do they both contract at the same speed? Are they producing equal amounts of tension?" Also, make sure that one or both shoulders are not involved in the exercise.

■ *5.2 During evaluation for proper initiation and bilateral symmetry, it is often helpful to close your eyes so as to get a "clean read" on muscle activity.*

Evaluating Unwanted Tension 3

Feel for unwanted tension in the upper trapezius muscle by placing your hands on those muscles in a maintained touch position (see Figure 5.3). It is sometimes difficult to detect this tension through visual observation alone.

■ *5.3 Evaluating for unwanted tension in the trapezius muscle.*

Evaluating Arm Position 3

Feel for arm position drift and/or the elbows wandering away from the sides of the body, as either of these will impede a maximal contraction. These slight shifts can be very subtle and difficult to detect.

Evaluating for a Controlled Eccentric Contraction 3

Feel for a smooth contraction on the downward movement of the curl until the arm is fully extended at the end of each repetition. Determine if your exerciser is "dropping" the weight rather than gradually lengthening the muscle.

4 | Instruction and Feedback

Now that you have observed and evaluated your exerciser performing the biceps curl, it is time to use the techniques that you learned in chapters 3 and 4 to make the necessary corrections. Most exercisers will not commit all of the errors we have listed all of the time. But if your exerciser is making many errors simultaneously, take your time and correct only one or two in each set. Allow time for the exerciser to absorb the change and establish the mind–body connection.

Body Alignment 4

Exercisers lifting free weights from a standing position often have incorrect body alignment. To correct these problems, supplement verbal instruction with touch. Use some or all of the techniques shown in Figure 5.4 to correct your exerciser's body alignment.

- Touch the back of the knee joint while you instruct your exerciser to keep her knees slightly bent (Figure 5.4a).
- Touch the iliac crests while you instruct her to keep her pelvis in neutral alignment (Figure 5.4b).
- Hold your finger approximately 1 to 2 inches from the sternum and ask her to move toward your finger until her body weight is drawn over the balls of her feet (Figure 5.4c).
- Palpate the rhomboids to correct slouching and touch the abdomen a quarter inch below the navel while instructing her to contract her abdominals to avoid arching backward (Figures 5.4d and 5.4e).

Initiation 4

Instruct your exerciser to tense the biceps before initiating the biceps curl.

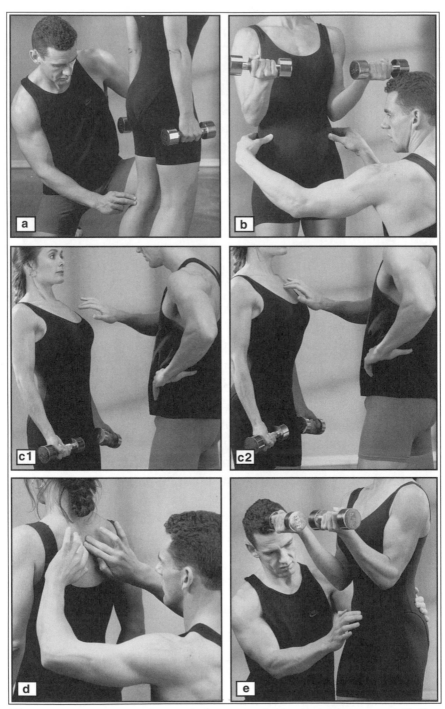

■ **5.4** Touching as you instruct helps correct body alignment more quickly than verbal cues alone. These photos illustrate some common corrections.

Bilateral Symmetry 4

If you detect a difference in the amount of tension between the left and the right biceps, stand behind your exerciser and cup both biceps. As illustrated in Figure 5.5, your little finger should be on the medial (inside) of the muscle, while the thumb should be on the lateral (outside). This placement of the hand forms a natural cup over the muscle. During the biceps curl, instruct your exerciser to try to "fill this cup with your muscle." This encourages her to create greater muscle tension where needed.

■ **5.5** *Forming a cup with both of your hands over the exerciser's biceps helps to ensure bilateral symmetry. The exerciser can feel the cup formed by your hands and tries to "fill" it by creating greater and/or equal tension in the biceps.*

Unwanted Tension 4

When performing the biceps curl, exercisers often develop inappropriate or unwanted tension in the hands, forearms, and trapezius.

Tight Handgrip.   Gripping the dumbbell too tightly instead of gently wrapping the hands around the weight can be corrected by touching lightly with your fingers to the back of your exerciser's hands while telling her to ease her grip.

Forearm Fatigue.   If after a set, you ask your exerciser, "Where did you feel this exercise working?" and she responds that she felt pain or fatigue in her forearms, instruct her to loosen her handgrip. In the next set, touch the forearms and the hand to remind her to stay relaxed. Then place your hands back on her biceps muscle belly to feel for renewed tension.

Trapezius Tension.   If during your evaluation you detect tension exerted inappropriately in the upper trapezius, place your hands with light to moderate pressure in a maintained touch position on both sides of the upper trapezius (Figure 5.6) and instruct your exerciser to release the tension beneath your hands (touch-to-relax).

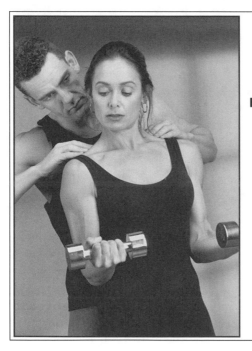

■ **5.6** *"Trapping" one's way through biceps curls is common. To direct more tension into the biceps and less into the trapezius muscle, use the "touch-to-relax" technique for about 2 to 3 seconds.*

Arm Position 4

Often during a set, your exerciser's elbows may begin to drift forward or backward and away from her sides. Rather than using your hands to hold her elbows in place, try standing behind her and placing two fingers on the medial (inside) edge of her elbows (Figure 5.7). Then instruct her to use her elbows to press *your* fingers into her sides.

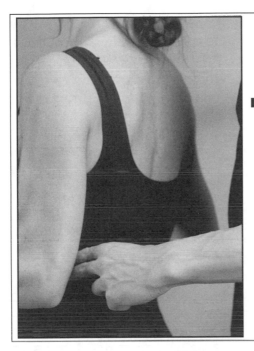

■ *5.7 To correct an exerciser's arm drift have her press trainer's fingers into her sides.*

Throwing the Weight 4

An exerciser who continually throws the weight up toward her shoulders and does not respond to verbal instructions can be helped by the stroking method. Slide two fingers up the biceps muscle from the elbow toward the shoulder at a pace more appropriate for the concentric portion of the curl. Instruct your exerciser to follow your rhythm to achieve a smooth contraction.

Cheating the Weight Up 4

Your exerciser may also "cheat" by rolling her shoulders slightly backward and scooping under or rocking the weight up. To correct this habit with the touch technique, stand in front of your exerciser and hold your index finger about 1 to 2 inches away from her sternum. Request that she move her sternum toward your finger until she has shifted her weight to the balls of her feet. Then help her to focus on contracting the biceps muscle smoothly and in the correct line of pull. If she is still unable to perform the exercise correctly (i.e., she can't create enough muscle tension throughout the full range of motion), try using the walking method. Beginning with the index and middle fingers on the muscle near the elbow, walk your fingers up the muscle toward her shoulder in the direction in which the muscle is shortening. This method directs the muscle contraction while providing important feedback to your exerciser about where the muscle should be contracting. The same positive results may be achieved with the stroking method. If you choose the walking method, stand to the side of your exerciser and work only one arm at a time. If you're stroking, stand behind your exerciser and work both arms simultaneously.

Wrists in Neutral Position 4

Loss of tension in the biceps can also be caused by unstable wrists that bend either forward or backward. Although a hyperextended wrist during a biceps curl sometimes denotes an advanced technique, it more often represents an unconscious error. To help your exerciser keep her wrists in a neutral position, stroke the opposite side to which the hand is bending and instruct her to straighten her wrist.

Maximizing the Concentric Contraction 4

To maximize a contraction at the top of the curl, walk or slide two fingers upward during the shortening (concentric) phase of the contraction and instruct your exerciser to squeeze her muscle at the top of the curl. Palpate with one finger the point to which you want her to reach (see Figure 5.8).

Controlling the Eccentric Contraction 4

If you detect your exerciser dropping the weight or lowering it too quickly, then during the next downward movement use

■ *5.8* *To create a target or goal for your exerciser during the biceps curl, palpate the point that you want her to reach during the concentric phase of the contraction.*

either the walking method or slide two fingers straight down the biceps muscle from the point of origin through the point of insertion at a pace more appropriate for the eccentric portion of the curl. Instruct her to follow your rhythm and to arc the weights out on the downward movement while keeping her elbows close to her body.

Delaying the Effects of Muscle Fatigue 4

Note that so far the causes we have listed for tension loss in the biceps can be classified as mechanical error. However, it is important to remember that one of the most common causes of tension loss in the muscle is the onset of muscle fatigue near the end of the set. While we are not certain of the exact explanation, we believe that STT, applied timely, can delay the effects of muscle fatigue. If your goal is to increase strength, you should specifically feel for signs of muscle fatigue; at the moment you detect its onset, instruct your exerciser to attempt to increase tension in all areas of the muscle. Encourage this process by applying the palpation/squeeze and stroking techniques at a slightly faster tempo to both the lateral and medial sides of the muscle belly to help facilitate the recruitment of additional motor units.

EXAMPLE TWO

MUSCLE TYPE
Quadriceps
(large round muscles)

EXERCISE
Seated
Leg Extensions
(machine)

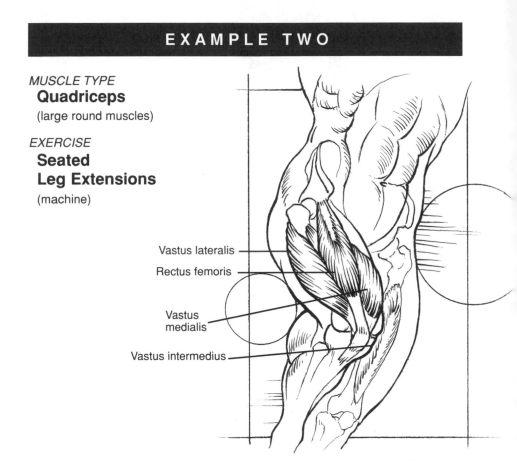

Vastus lateralis

Rectus femoris

Vastus medialis

Vastus intermedius

1 | Warm Up and Observation

The leg extension has become so standard that it is often performed mindlessly. Touch changes that and helps reunite the mind and the body. After your exerciser has warmed up and stretched, observe while he performs seated leg extensions for several repetitions. Here are some of the more common errors you may detect during observation of the seated leg extension:

- "Kicking out" or jerking the lower legs
- Locking or hyperextending the knee when extending the legs
- Rocking or using momentum to move the weight
- Rounding of the lower back
- Arching of the lower back
- Sunken chest
- Leaning to a favored (stronger) side
- One leg starting before the other (taking on more weight)
- Holding the breath through the exercise
- Tension in the upper trapezius muscles
- Tight handgrip causing tension in the arms and neck

2 | Explanation

Describe the characteristics of the muscles to your exerciser by briefly discussing

- what the muscles do,
- where they are located,
- where they attach to the bone, and
- the line of pull.

Touch the muscles while you explain these characteristics. Although the quadriceps are easy to isolate and are most often used correctly, still include all of the steps of the STT process when using the technique for the first time or when working with a beginner.

Muscle Description 2

You may wish to offer the following explanation.

Rectus Femoris.   The quadriceps are a group of four muscles located in the front of the thigh. The function of all four is to lift the lower leg by extending the knee. One of the four is the rectus femoris, which runs down the center of the thigh. It crosses the hip joint as well as the knee joint and thus helps in flexing the hip. (Because the rectus femoris is long and large, use a three- or four-finger stroking technique [Figure 5.9] to

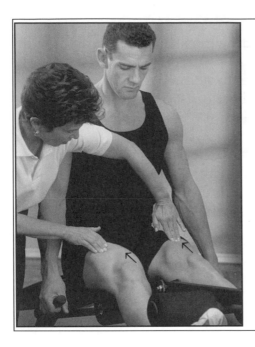

■ **5.9** *Identify the rectus femoris by stroking from the point of insertion back toward the point of origin.*

identify it from the point of insertion back toward the point of origin).

Vastus Medialis, Vastus Lateralis, and Vastus Intermedius.

The other three muscles of the quadriceps originate at different levels along the femur (thigh bone). The teardrop-shaped vastus medialis lies just above and to the inside of the knee (palpate with one to three fingers as shown in Figure 5.10 as you point out and describe this muscle). The vastus lateralis is a longer sweeping muscle that lies to the outside of the thigh and gives it a distinctive, shapely "cut" (use the knife-edge technique as shown in Figure 5.11 to run the lateral edge of your palm along this muscle's outer borders). The vastus intermedius lies deep beneath the rectus femoris and cannot be palpated.

Explain to your exerciser the importance of isolating each of these muscles during the workout. Using light weight allows him to concentrate on technique rather than on the amount of weight being lifted. Explain also the importance of keeping the strength of these four muscles well balanced because they

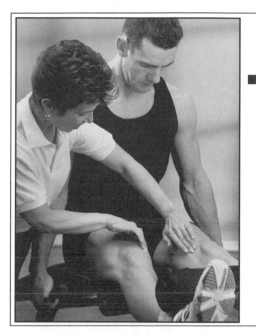

■ *5.10* *Palpate with one to three fingers as you outline and describe the teardrop-shaped vastus medialis while the exerciser tries to contract this muscle.*

■ *5.11* *Identify the vastus lateralis by using your hand in a knife-edge position along its outside border.*

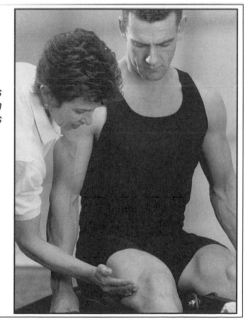

act to keep the patella (kneecap) properly placed, which helps to avoid injury.

Fiber Direction.   The quadriceps consist of muscle fibers all running in the same direction—from their attachments along the femur to their insertion at the knee. All four muscles blend into a common quadriceps tendon that inserts into the patella and from the patella to the tibia.

Movements Involving the Quadriceps 2

These muscles are used in cycling and in all jumping and kicking activities, such as volleyball, basketball, and soccer. The rectus femoris also aids hip flexion in sports such as water and downhill skiing.

3 | Evaluation

Begin your evaluation of the leg extension exercises by standing to the side of the exerciser and using the maintained touch technique, placing both hands over the lower portion of each quadriceps (see Figure 5.12). Feel the vastus medialis with your thumbs, the vastus lateralis with your forefingers, and the rectus femoris with the heel of your palms. Depending on your height and size and that of your exerciser, as well as the placement of the machinery, you may have to modify your STT techniques to avoid awkward body mechanics that put you at risk for injury.

During the evaluation and/or the instruction and feedback phases of the quadriceps exercise, you could use the following methods of touch:

- Maintained touch
- Knife-edge
- Walking
- Stroking

- Palpation/squeeze
- Touch-to-relax
- Phantom fingers

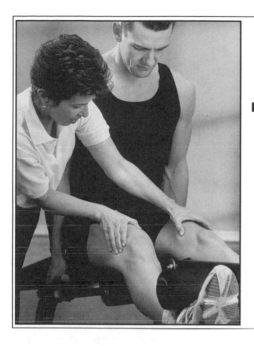

■ *5.12 Evaluate tension in the quadriceps by standing to the side of the exerciser and touching as much of the lower part of the muscle as your hands can cover.*

Evaluating Body Alignment 3

Most body alignment problems that occur during the seated quadriceps extension can be observed visually, so a hands-on evaluation is not necessary. Provide verbal instructions along with hands-on corrections. Use weight slightly lighter than what your exerciser is accustomed to. This way you can be sure that his form and technique are perfect before you allow him to progress to a heavier weight.

Evaluating Initiation 3

Ask your exerciser to begin extending his legs as you feel for the initiation of the contraction deep within the quadriceps muscle. It is quite common for the exerciser to kick out before first contracting the quadriceps. Before the actual movement takes place, feel for tension in the quadriceps by using maintained touch or a light palpation/squeeze technique.

Evaluating Bilateral Symmetry 3

Using maintained touch over the center of both the right and left quadriceps groups, feel for unequal strength. Often your exerciser will lift with one leg before the other or lift the weight unequally. Using STT, you will be able to determine if one leg is exerting more force than the other. Through hands-on evaluation you can also find "dead spots." Continue by palpating and using maintained touch over the entire quadriceps muscle to determine whether the exerciser is recruiting all parts of the muscle to perform the leg extension. Feel for equal contraction of the right and left vastus medialis and the right and left vastus lateralis.

Evaluating Unwanted Tension 3

Touch the forearms to determine whether the exerciser's grip is so tight that it creates too much tension in the forearm and hands and therefore less in the quadriceps. Note that when using a very heavy weight, a tight handgrip may be unavoidable. Also touch the upper trapezius to feel for unwanted tension.

Evaluating the Vastus Medialis and Vastus Lateralis 3

For a more detailed evaluation ask your exerciser to contract his quadriceps so that you can test the strength of both the vastus lateralis and the vastus medialis. Evaluate each muscle separately using maintained touch or the palpation/squeeze method with moderate intensity.

4 Instruction and Feedback

Now that you have observed and evaluated your exerciser performing the seated leg extension, it is time to use the techniques that you learned in chapters 3 and 4 to make the necessary corrections.

Body Alignment 4

To correct a sunken chest and rounded lower back, palpate your exerciser's sternum. Then leave one finger barely touching the sternum and instruct him to lift his chest into your touch (Figure 5.13a). Next, palpate the abdominal muscles as you instruct him to tense them and sit up straight (Figure 5.13b). This should take the arch out of the low back.

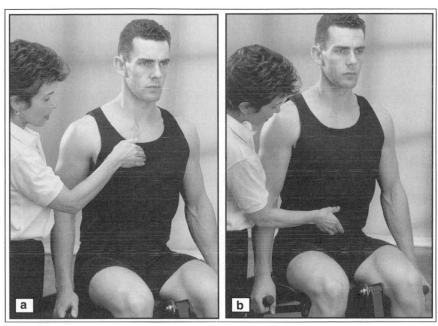

■ *5.13 Use touch to correct a sunken chest and/or a rounded back. Ask your exerciser to lift his chest into your touch (a) and to contract and pull in his abdominals as you touch them (b).*

Initiation 4

Instruct your exerciser to begin his leg extension by first contracting the quadriceps. His hamstrings and gluteals will likely tighten also, but do not allow them to dominate the exercise. Ask the exerciser to imagine pulling his kneecap "up toward his thigh" and allow the lower leg to "almost float out" as a result. To aid this imagery, stroke firmly upward, starting just above the patella. Once you feel tension in the quadriceps, use both the palpation/squeeze and a firm stroking technique to intensify the tension.

Bilateral Symmetry 4

If you detect that one quadriceps is working more than the other, concentrate on using the appropriate STT techniques on the weaker leg to restore equal tension. Use basic palpation and/or the squeeze variation in a long, stroking motion to achieve equality. Work the specific muscles and "dead spots" with a moderate to firm intensity because this is a large and thick muscle that responds well to more aggressive stroking. Once the quadriceps have achieved equal tension, instruct your exerciser to work the two quadriceps together for the last few repetitions.

Unwanted Tension 4

If you see or feel helper muscles being inappropriately used, ask your exerciser to relax and release those muscles and to focus on using the quadriceps. Verbal instruction accompanied by a light touch on the upper trapezius, forearms, or hands (touch-to-relax technique) usually eliminates the tension. Many exercisers contract their hamstrings and gluteals too tightly before each repetition. This tension may help them lift a heavier weight, but it does not help them to isolate the quadriceps. Lighten the weight, then stroke and palpate the quadriceps while instructing your exerciser to try to relax the gluteals.

Kickout 4

To control kickout and eliminate the use of momentum, use the palpation/squeeze technique to firmly stroke the quadriceps muscles in a long, slow motion. This helps your exerciser refocus his attention from kicking out the foot to contracting the quadriceps. There is a subtle but important difference.

Delaying the Effects of Muscle Fatigue 4

To encourage the exerciser to continue holding the contraction and to delay fatigue, perform a series of stroking and palpating motions both to the vastus medialis and lateralis to help recruit additional muscle fibers. Stroke and palpate the lateral and medial sides of the specific muscles, as it is usually in these locations that additional motor units can be recruited. This technique should be employed with slightly greater intensity and speed because the quadriceps are a large muscle group with more surface area to cover.

EXAMPLE THREE

MUSCLE TYPE
Latissimus Dorsi
(large flat muscles)

EXERCISE
**Wide Grip
Lat Pull-Down**

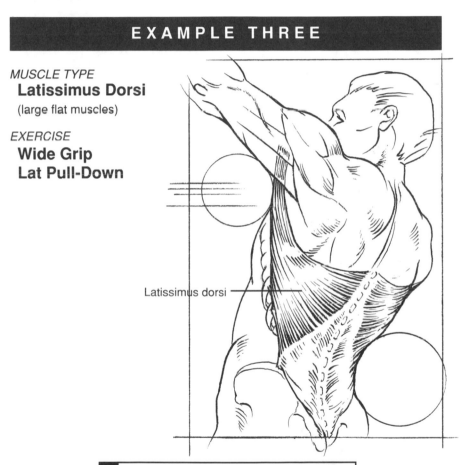

Latissimus dorsi

1 Warm Up and Observation

The same general format we used earlier with the biceps brachii and quadriceps can be followed for the latissimus dorsi. First, watch your exerciser complete several repetitions of the pull-down in his warm-up set without providing instruction or feedback. Look for proper body alignment, form, and technique, as these are all essential to the effectiveness of this exercise.

These are some common errors you may detect during observation of the wide grip latissimus pull-down.

- Failure to properly position the body directly under the overhead bar
- Raising the heels off the floor and using the toes for support
- Jerking or snapping motions to pull the bar down
- Pulling initially from the arms, not the back
- Excessive rocking of the torso and using the momentum to pull the weight down
- Allowing the head and neck to drop too far forward to touch the bar to the back of the neck
- Rounding out the lower back
- Allowing the weight to snap back upward to the starting position, thereby losing control of the eccentric contraction
- Bouncing off the seat
- Failure to release tension in the upper trapezius muscles
- Gripping hands too tightly around the bar
- Hyperextending the shoulder joint to force the bar to touch the midback
- Allowing the elbows to drift forward

2 Explaining Muscle Makeup

When I begin working with a new exerciser, regardless of his fitness level, I always review some of the characteristics of the target muscle, including its location, the attachments to bone, the direction of muscle pull, and its function. I usually touch the skin over the muscle with my index finger or outline it with a skin pencil while I am describing these features.

Muscle Description 2

You may wish to provide the following explanation.

Latissimus Dorsi. The latissimus dorsi is a large muscle that covers the middle and lower portions of the back. It originates at the lower spine on the crest of the ilium and spans the vertebrae from the lumbar region to T7 (touch the ilium as shown in Figure 5.14a). It attaches to the upper arm on the front side of the humerus (touch the humerus as shown in Figure 5.14b). The latissimus dorsi has more surface area than any other muscle, and because it is fan-shaped when fully developed, it gives the torso a desirable V-shape. When performing the wide grip pull-down, the latissimus is responsible for pulling the arms downward and backward toward the spine.

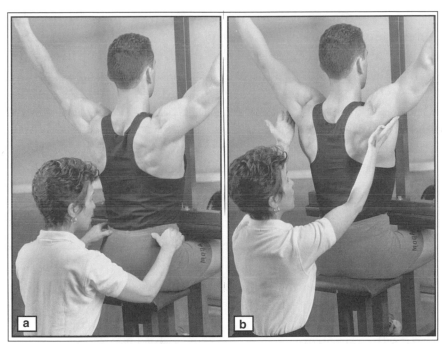

■ **5.14** *During muscle description, touch the area of origin (a) and insertion (b). For a large muscle, like the latissimus, use the broad hand to sweep the muscle from the beginning point to its end point.*

Trapezius and Rhomboids. It is important to note that in the latissimus pull-down the trapezius muscle, along with the rhomboids, teres major, teres minor, and infraspinatus will also be engaged. The trapezius and rhomboids pull the shoulder blades toward the spine. The teres major, teres minor, and infraspinatus pull the arm in toward the shoulder blade. Other helper muscles involved in the latissimus pull-down include the biceps, the posterior deltoid, and the erector spinae.

Fiber Direction.   The latissimus and trapezius are both fan-shaped muscles and contract along several lines, whereas the other muscles involved in the pull-down are parallel and contract only along one line. Whether the exerciser is executing a wide grip, narrow grip, or any variation of the latissimus pull-down, these muscles will be involved at one time or another and you will want to understand their line of pull.

Palpating the muscle in the appropriate place during the exercise facilitates the most effective use of the muscle and helps engage as many fibers as possible. When outlining the latissimus with your finger or a skin pencil, be sure to emphasize the different lines of force that make up the latissimus. While explaining the latissimus pull-down, you should emphasize only one of those directions—that is, the one that is nearly straight and slightly diagonal from top to bottom. With variations of body position and arm position, however, all of the muscle fibers can be stimulated. To fully develop the latissimus, you must work along all lines of contraction.

Movements Involving the Latissimus Muscle **2**

The powerful latissimus muscle is used primarily in activities that draw the upper arm (humerus) and torso together, such as the swimming breaststroke, paddling a canoe, and rowing. When the arms are fixed, however, such as when hanging on a bar, it is the latissimus that raises the body, as in a chin-up or a rope climb. These various functions of the muscle will come into play as you move through the latissimus exercises.

3 Evaluation

You can use hands-on evaluation techniques to detect bilateral muscle imbalances and overinvolvement of synergists and to determine if the exerciser is using the appropriate muscle to perform the exercise. Begin your evaluation of the latissimus pull-down by kneeling on one knee to maintain your own balance.

During the evaluation and/or the instruction and feedback phases of the latissimus dorsi exercise, you may want to use some or all of the following methods of touch:

- Maintained touch
- Stroking
- Palpation
- Touch-to-relax

Evaluating Body Alignment 3

Observe if your exerciser is seated in proper body alignment directly under the machine, with the retaining bar securely across his knees and his feet planted flat on the floor.

Evaluating Initiation 3

Prior to the movement, monitor the tension in the muscle by placing your hands in a maintained touch position on the upper latissimus. If you detect that the movement is being initiated with the arms instead of the back, leave your hands in the same position and instruct your exerciser to initiate the movement from the upper portion of the latissimus by retracting the scapulae in and down. Do not allow your exerciser to continue a pull-down until you feel the movement beneath your hands. Often he is not aware that he is bending his elbows and pulling with the biceps. Place your hands on the back of his elbows to give him a point of reference (Figure 5.15). Instruct him not to bend his elbows but to keep them straight until you give him instructions to bend. These tactile cues are almost always effective.

Evaluating Bilateral Symmetry 3

Check whether the left and right latissimus are producing equal tension. To do this, use maintained touch with the entire hand in contact with the skin over the muscle (Figure 5.16). One way to confirm bilateral symmetry is to determine whether the two scapulae come together during the exercise. If the two latissimi are contracting equivalently, the scapulae should almost touch

■ *5.15 For the exerciser who is unaware that he initiates the pull-down by bending his elbows, touch the back of the elbows as a tactile cue while instructing him to keep them straight.*

near the spine. If they do not, use maintained touch during the exercise to determine which of the sides is contracting less (Figure 5.17).

Evaluating Unwanted Tension 3

Trapezius. Using maintained touch, evaluate the upper trapezius muscle for tension. Very often your exercisers will work from the upper trapezius to the exclusion of the middle and lower segments. The upper trapezius is the most likely area of tension during a latissimus pull-down. By simply touching lightly the upper trapezius and instructing your exerciser to release the tension from this muscle (touch-to-relax), the tension in the upper trapezius will usually move down into the middle and lower trapezius and the latissimus (see Figure 5.18). To verify that your exerciser is now producing more tension within the latissimus, slide your hands to the outer edge of the upper latissimus and feel for renewed tension.

■ **5.16** *To evaluate bilateral symmetry of the right and left latissimus, use maintained touch.*

■ **5.17** *Another technique for evaluating equal tension is to determine whether both scapulae come together near the spine.*

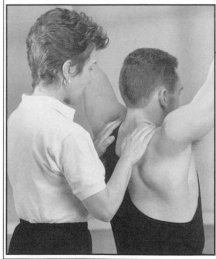

■ **5.18** *Use the touch-to-relax technique to relieve unwanted tension during a lat pull-down.*

Handgrip. If you are still not getting the tension in the latissimus muscle that you deem appropriate for the exerciser's level, examine the exerciser's handgrip by placing your hand on top of his to see how much tension he is exerting while holding the bar. You should be able to relax the handgrip by touching the top of his hand lightly and telling him to loosen his grip. You will often feel renewed strength being directed into the latissimus.

Evaluating Shoulder Girdle Retraction 3

In evaluating shoulder girdle retraction (scapula moving toward spine), simply palpate the middle trapezius and rhomboids with your fingers (palpation technique) to make sure this action is taking place.

Evaluating Lower Latissimus Involvement 3

To make sure that the lower latissimus is engaged, slide your hands toward the lower portion of the latissimus (closer to the waist). You can feel the muscle activity at the base or origin of the muscle, which is the crest of the ilium, by placing your hand slightly above the crest as shown in Figure 5.19. You

■ *5.19 Feel for initiation of the contraction near the crest of the ilium.*

should feel your exerciser contract his latissimus at this level, arch his back slightly, contract his abdominals (you can feel for this, if necessary, by placing your flat hand on the abdominals), and then initiate the pull. Immediately following evaluation of all these points, offer instruction and feedback as to what you felt, or did not feel, and the way to correct or continue to produce the appropriate movement.

4 | Instruction and Feedback

Now that you have observed and evaluated your exerciser performing the wide grip latissimus pull-down, it is once again time to use the techniques that you learned in chapters 3 and 4 to make the necessary corrections.

Body Alignment 4

If you see your exerciser lift his heels and balance on his toes, lightly touch his calves and instruct him to relax these muscles. His feet should remain flat on the floor.

Initiation and Line of Pull 4

Following evaluation, stroke the latissimus along its line of pull to give your exerciser the direction of the muscle contraction. As the muscle is large, this stroking should be done with a broad hand. Make sure that his muscles contract throughout their entire range of motion and that the initiation of the movement is with the latissimus and not with the arms (Figure 5.20).

Bilateral Symmetry 4

If the scapulae do not come together, then instruct your exerciser to engage them while you palpate the scapula that is not fully contracting.

Unwanted Tension—Biceps, Forearms, and Hands 4

If your exerciser complains of fatigue in his biceps and forearms at the end of a set, try to use a light relaxing touch (touch-to-relax technique) on the biceps, forearms, and hands along

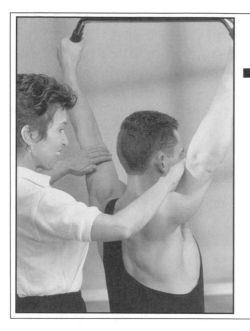

■ *5.20 If you detect excessive biceps involvement at the beginning of the movement, use the touch-to-relax technique.*

with verbal instructions. This should ease the tension and also smooth out any jerking or snapping movements.

Arm Position 4

Once your exerciser is able to effectively initiate the latissimus pull-down with his back rather than his arms, touch his elbows to give him a tactile point of reference, which helps him focus his attention and guide his elbows backward and outward. These tactile cues along with verbal instructions help to keep the latissimus tensed and the elbows back while descending into the latissimus pull. You should continue to intermittently palpate the area of the skin covering the middle trapezius, rhomboids, teres major and minor, and infraspinatus to ensure that the shoulder blades are pulled toward the spine during the contraction (see Figure 5.21a). Then, using the heels of your hands, stroke from the posterior deltoids upward to just below the exerciser's elbows to encourage a slow and complete return to the starting position before he begins the next repetition (see Figure 5.21b).

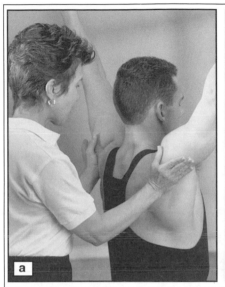
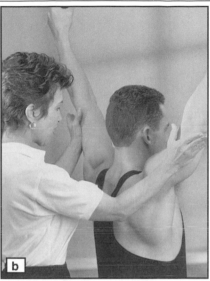

■ **5.21** *Place the heels of your hands firmly under the posterior deltoids (a) and move them upward between the shoulders and elbows as the exerciser returns to the starting position (b).*

Lower Latissimus Involvement 4

To be sure that the lower portion of the latissimus is properly engaged, palpate the muscle at its proximal insertion (crest of the ilium) and wait until you feel muscle tension. This forces the back to arch slightly. Instruct your exerciser to tense his abdominal muscles. Next, place the middle fingers of both your hands just below the rib cage bilaterally. At the same time, leave the thumbs touching the crest of the ilium (see Figure 5.22a). Then draw your thumbs and middle fingers together to give your exerciser information about the direction of pull (Figure 5.22b). This has proved to be a very useful technique, as it is often difficult for exercisers to engage the lower latissimus.

Stretching the Shoulder Girdle 4

To encourage a full stretch during the beginning of the exercise, instruct your exerciser to feel the stretch in the latissimus and to feel his scapula move out away from the spine as far as

■ *5.22* To encourage lower latissimus involvement, palpate (a) and slide together the first three fingers and thumbs (b) to give the exerciser information about the direction of the pull.

possible. Very often, the stretch takes place mainly in the shoulder joint and not in the latissimus. To facilitate a better stretch, place your open hands lightly on the part of the latissimus you want to stretch, and then use maintained touch until you feel the muscles release beneath your hands. If your exerciser is able to "let go" and relax the muscle, give him appropriate and encouraging feedback. This technique also eliminates bouncing off the seat during the eccentric phase. All exercisers can learn to do a latissimus pull-down, but they will learn much more quickly with the use of touch.

Establishing Rhythm 4

As with all forms of exercise, rhythm is important when performing the latissimus pull-down. You can set a comfortable tempo by stroking the muscle with an open hand. Most exercisers tend to cut short both the stretching portion and the pull-down portion of the movement. You can help your exerciser through the full range of motion by stroking up and then down the outside edge of the latissimus, starting from the crest of the ilium and moving up to the top of the humerus.

Head Drop 4

When fatigued, an exerciser will often drop his head or hunch forward excessively. If this occurs, touch the muscles at the back of the neck on either side of the spine while instructing your exerciser to pull his head back into a neutral position. This gives him a tactile cue as to what muscles to use to correct his form. You are also able to better evaluate whether he is using these muscles. Continue to palpate until the appropriate muscle response takes place.

Preserving Good Form 4

Use lighter weights to preserve good form and obtain more effective results. If the weight is too heavy, your exerciser will rely on momentum and the muscles of the hip, lower back, or arms to move the weight. You should also remind your exerciser that it is easier to engage his lower latissimus if he contracts his abdominal muscles first.

Delaying the Effects of Muscle Fatigue 4

After your exerciser has developed good technique, focus your efforts on improving the overall strength of his muscle. This is generally done as the muscle is fatiguing. Just as with the biceps brachii, you should evaluate the final 2 or 3 repetitions in a 10-repetition set for decreasing tension. When you detect decreasing tension, palpate the upper latissimus using two or three fingers. You'll need to move your fingers rapidly to cover the large area. Then, with both hands placed flat on your exerciser's back and your fingertips pointing away from you, stroke in a downward and inward direction on the latissimus at an intensity slightly more than moderate. Stroke inward (horizontally) on the upper back muscles as well. This additional tactile input helps the exerciser to maintain the muscle tension a little longer. The most common feedback I receive from exercisers doing latissimus work is that STT keeps them totally focused and "in touch" with their back. They tell me they can actually feel their muscles follow the directions my hands provide, almost as if they were being guided along a pathway.

EXAMPLE FOUR

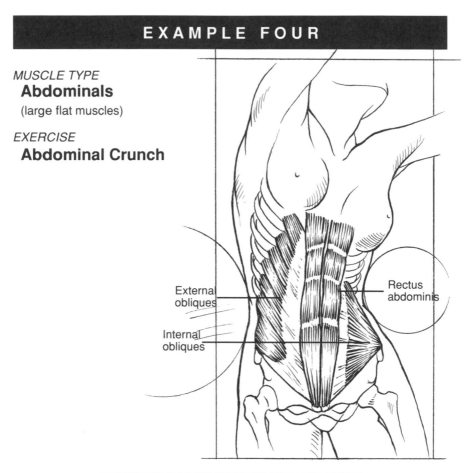

MUSCLE TYPE
Abdominals
(large flat muscles)

EXERCISE
Abdominal Crunch

External obliques

Internal obliques

Rectus abdominis

1 Warm Up and Observation

After the warm-up and stretch, ask your exerciser to perform two or three of the abdominal exercises that she uses in her regular routine. Pay close attention to her form, looking for signs of faulty technique. Later, use your hands to verify your observations.

Here are some common errors you may detect during observation of the abdominal crunch:

- Incorrect breathing patterns
- Losing control by moving too quickly through the contraction and release phases
- Using momentum or throwing the legs up
- Pulling the head, neck, and shoulder with the arms
- Overinvolvement of the hip flexors
- Excessive pelvic tilt or lordotic curve
- Failure to isolate specific abdominal muscles
- Causing strain on the neck muscles by jutting the chin forward or pressing the chin to the neck
- Resting too long between repetitions

2 Explanation

Before beginning your explanation of the abdominal muscles (including their function, location, attachments to the bone, and their line of pull), decide whether you will outline the locations on your body or on the exerciser's. Although it is helpful to use your exerciser's body, under some circumstances it may be wiser to use your own body for demonstration, especially if you're working with the opposite gender or with someone who would rather not be touched in such a sensitive area.

As always, please remember to inform your exerciser that you are going to touch, why you are touching, and exactly where you will touch. You might say, "I am going to palpate the lower abdominals just below the navel to determine if you're using these muscles to initiate the movement or if you're using your hip flexors to do the work."

The abdominal muscles are complex, with several layers lying in different directions and functions both diverse and overlapping, so be sure to keep your explanation simple and clear, especially for beginners.

Muscle Description 2

You may wish to offer the following explanation. The abdominal muscles are large, flat muscles that lie in four layers and extend in several directions. They consist of the rectus abdominis, the external and internal obliques, and the transverse abdominis.

For the Beginning Exerciser. The rectus abdominis lies in a vertical plane and is involved in bending the body forward or sideways. It bends the torso forward by drawing the pelvis and the rib cage together. The internal and external obliques allow the body to bend to the side and to rotate. If the obliques are both contracted at the same time, they also help in forward flexion. The transverse abdominis, the deepest muscle of the four, wraps around the torso like a cummerbund. Unlike the other three that produce flexion and extension of the vertebral column, this muscle is responsible for forced expiration caused by the tightening of the abdominal wall, and it helps keep all of your internal organs intact.

(I have found it highly effective to provide this simple explanation while I touch and outline the location of the muscle and the line of pull. The information along with the touch immediately improves the exerciser's ability to focus and to contract her abdominal muscles properly when executing any one of the exercises.)

For the Advanced Exerciser. For more advanced exercisers, you may want to explain in more detail to help them visualize the origin and insertion points as well as the muscle function. Abdominal work can become mindless and robotic because we do so many repetitions. I find that the more information I provide, the better my exercisers stay focused. I suggest that you include some or all of the following in your explanation.

Rectus Abdominis. The rectus abdominis is a long, slender muscle located in the center of the abdominal wall that extends vertically from the pubic bone to the sternum. It originates on the crest of the pubis and inserts on the cartilages of the fifth, sixth, and seventh ribs. It is composed of fibers running vertically and is crossed horizontally by three tendinous intersections. These intersections give the "ripped" or "washboard" look to abdominals that have been well worked.

Although it is common to refer to the upper and lower abdominals, they are not really separate but are opposite ends of the same muscle running the entire length of the torso. Specific exercises increase the muscle contraction in both areas, however, and it feels as if two separate muscles are working. Even though flexion of the spine is the main function of the rectus abdominis, the muscle is not attached to the spine. Movement occurs because of the pull of the rib cage and the pelvis drawing together during contraction.

External and Internal Obliques.   The external and internal obliques are attached in several places. The fibers of the external oblique run on a downward diagonal to form a large V. The external oblique originates on the external surface of ribs 5 through 12 and inserts on the front half of the crest of the ilium, the crest of the pubis, and the linea alba.

Lying deep and directly below the external obliques are the internal obliques, which originate on the lumbar fascia and the anterior crest of the ilium, inserting at ribs 9 through 12 and at the linea alba. These muscles run upward on a diagonal and form an inverted V. The internal and external obliques help to compress the internal organs and allow the torso to laterally bend, rotate, and flex forward.

Transverse Abdominis.   The transverse abdominis is the fourth layer of the abdominal wall and lies immediately below the internal obliques. It is made up of parallel fibers running horizontally across the abdomen. Fibers of the transverse abdominis form a cummerbund-like band around the torso. Originating along the lumbar vertebral fascia, it generally outlines the rib cage as well as the pelvic girdle and inserts along the linea alba. The function of the transverse abdominis is to help hold the internal organs in place. Unlike the other abdominal muscles, it does not flex the vertebral column.

Fiber Direction.   Here is a quick review of the fiber direction of each of the abdominal muscles.

- *Rectus abdominis:* straight up and down from pelvis to sternum
- *External obliques:* diagonal from ribs to pelvis
- *Internal obliques:* diagonal from the crest of the ilium to the ribs
- *Transverse abdominis:* horizontal parallel fibers from the lumbar fascia to the linea alba

Movements Involving the Abdominal Muscles 2

The strong, multifunctional abdominal muscles are used primarily in activities that require bending forward (gymnastics and diving), rotating and twisting (golfing and throwing the discus or javelin), and bending sideways (canoeing or playing polo).

3 Evaluation

Before starting your hands-on evaluation in the sensitive abdominal area, always let your exerciser perform a few repetitions without touch. Then tell her which abdominal muscles you are going to touch. Ask her to stop and start again so that you can feel for the initiation of the contraction. This seems to make the touch less startling, allowing for a smoother approach to evaluation. Hands-on evaluation and correction work particularly well with the abdominal muscles. I find that it is sometimes easier to get a "clean read" if I work slowly with my eyes closed.

During the evaluation and/or the instruction and feedback phases of the abdominal exercises, you may use the following methods of touch:

- Maintained touch
- Stroking
- Palpation
- Touch-to-relax
- Phantom fingers

Evaluating Body Alignment 3

Have your exerciser lie in a supine position with knees bent. Instruct her to take one or two deep breaths and to slowly exhale before beginning the exercise. Before allowing her to begin the crunches, place the heels of your hands on her hips and rock her gently from side to side to relieve tension and to make sure she is in proper alignment. Then instruct her to begin her abdominal work as you evaluate.

Evaluating Initiation 3

Use the maintained touch technique to evaluate the amount of tension in the muscle prior to movement. The abdominal muscles—not the neck, shoulders, arms, or hip flexors—should initiate the movement. Feel for rib cage contraction at the beginning of exhalation, and evaluate any back arch. Check that both the "upper" and "lower" abdominals are engaged (see Figure 5.23). Touch the hip flexors to be sure that your exerciser does not use them to initiate the pull, but uses the lower abdominals.

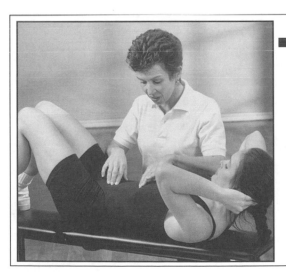

■ *5.23 Evaluate for initiation of movement in the lower abdomen by touching about 1 inch below the navel. You should feel the "lower" rectus abdominis rolling down and back away from your touch. Evaluate for initiation of movement in the "upper" rectus abdominis by feeling the ribs moving closer together and the muscle tightening under your fingers.*

Evaluating Bilateral Symmetry 3

Standing or kneeling at your exerciser's side, position your body at a slight diagonal facing her head. With your thumbs spread away from the forefingers and fingers wrapped around the front of the rib cage, your entire hand should be placed on your exerciser's abdominals, covering as much surface as possible (Figure 5.24). This way you can tell if both sides are contracting equally.

Evaluating Unwanted Tension 3

Unnecessary tension inhibits proper execution of abdominal contractions, so you'll want to check for unwanted tension in the quadriceps, arms, neck, and trapezius. A light touch to these areas will generally confirm your observations. Along with your verbal instruction to relax and release this tension, the touch may be all it takes for a stronger abdominal contraction. If not, remedy this problem during the instruction and feedback phase.

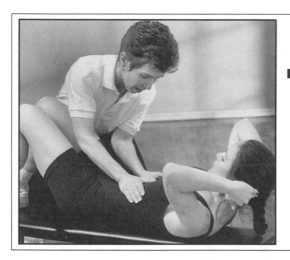

■ *5.24 Use maintained touch, covering as much of the abdominal surface as possible, to evaluate bilateral symmetry.*

Evaluating for Contraction of the Transverse Abdominis ■3

Ask your exerciser to perform an isometric contraction by contracting the transverse abdominis. Some say that the transverse abdominis lies too deep in the abdominal wall to be palpated, but I believe you may be able to feel it working along with the obliques covering it. Use maintained touch on either side of the abdominals and feel for isolated tension before flexion.

Evaluating the Rotation of the Torso ■3

With a maintained touch, you should feel the exerciser's obliques to confirm that any rotation during oblique work is originating in those muscles and not from a rolling or twisting movement of the shoulders.

Evaluating Muscle Imbalances ■3

Ask your exerciser if she is currently involved in any sports. Her answer might help you detect possible muscle imbalances involving the abdominals. Overdeveloped hip flexors and underdeveloped abdominals, for example, is a classic problem for runners and cyclists. They may complain of back problems and tell their trainers that they do extensive abdominal work. But very often they are using the hip flexors and not the abdominal muscles when exercising. Hands-on evaluation during abdominal repetitions should reveal this problem. During evaluation, ask your exerciser to demonstrate a crunch with a twist.

■4 Instruction and Feedback

Before beginning instruction, break the abdominal crunch down into segments so that your exerciser understands what is expected of her. I have found that abdominal work requires continuous evaluation to ensure that exercisers are interpreting instructions correctly.

Body Alignment 4

Place your exerciser in a neutral spine position. Some trainers try to correct back arch during abdominal work by placing a hand on the lumbar spine and instructing the exerciser to push her back into the hand. I find it more helpful to tell exercisers to *push* the lower back closer to the floor by *pulling* the abdominals in and down. Palpate the abdominals to help the exerciser focus and engage the proper muscles. Done properly, this will create a stretch in the low back and relax a hyperextended back.

Initiation 4

Place your exerciser in a neutral spine position. As she begins a set of crunches, feel for the correct initiation of the contraction. Feel first for the contraction that engages the "lower" rectus abdominis (two-fingered maintained touch), then check the "upper" rectus abdominis (two-fingered maintained touch), and, finally, feel the obliques (flat-hand maintained touch). If you do not feel the initiation of the contraction in each of these specific areas, palpate the area and tell the exerciser to tense that part of the muscle before moving any other body part (see Figure 5.25a and b).

Bilateral Symmetry 4

If you feel one side of the abdominals pulling harder than the other, use the open-handed maintained touch position to palpate the less active side until you feel the muscle respond to the stimulation. Then, using the stroking method, *drag* the increased tension down the length of the muscle to its endpoint. You will probably lose the contraction along the way. The tension vanishes, and the muscle may feel as if it has stopped responding. But the more you palpate and stroke specific areas, the more improvement you are likely to achieve during each set. After getting the weaker side to respond, I like to end the set by stroking both sides of the abdominals simultaneously.

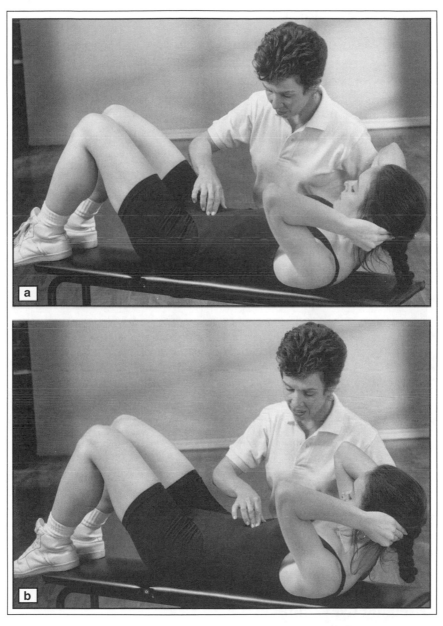

■ *5.25* To stimulate the use of the entire rectus abdominis, palpate with two or three fingers the various areas of the muscle . Begin palpation with the "lower" rectus abdominis (a). Then move to the "upper" rectus abdominis, fingers centered directly under the xyphoid process (b). With each subsequent palpation, slightly widen the fingers as you move downward again along the muscle.

Unwanted Tension 4

The most common areas of unwanted tension during abdominal work are the quadriceps, arms, neck, and trapezius (Figure 5.26a). If your exerciser continues to tense any one or all of these muscles during the crunch, use the touch-to-relax technique more aggressively.

Using the palpation/squeeze, gently shake the tensed quadriceps for about 2 seconds (Figure 5.26b). Use intensity level 2 to 3 while instructing the exerciser to release the tension. Once the unwanted tension has been released, return to the abdominals to check for renewed tension.

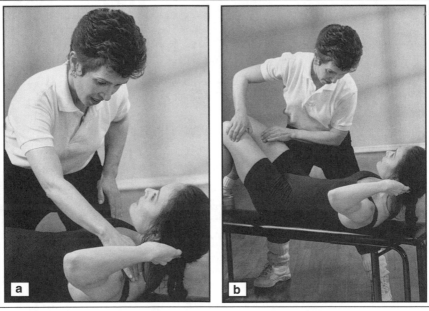

■ *5.26 Evaluate for unwanted tension in the trapezius (a) and the quadriceps (b) and redirect tension to the abdominals using touch-to-relax.*

Directing the Contraction 4

Once the contraction has been initiated, help your exerciser move into a full contraction by first palpating at the origins of the contraction and then stroking along the line in which the muscle contracts (Figure 5.27). Stroking with the first three

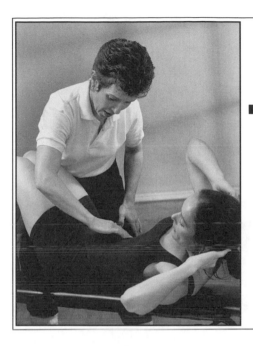

■ *5.27* Using three fingers, help direct the contraction by first palpating the origin of the muscle contraction then stroking along the line of pull.

fingers held closely together seems to work best in providing direction to the contraction. Try to stroke in rhythm with the exerciser's breathing pattern. After using this technique a few times, try maintained touch to evaluate if the exerciser is indeed contracting along the correct line of pull. The palpation technique immediately followed by stroking seems to work best.

Touching the Trainer 4

This next technique, if you feel comfortable with it, gives you an opportunity to demonstrate to your exerciser what the movement should feel like. Place the exerciser's hand on your abdominal muscles so she can feel how *you* initiate and complete a proper abdominal contraction (Figure 5.28). Feeling your muscles responding properly makes it easier for her to duplicate the movement.

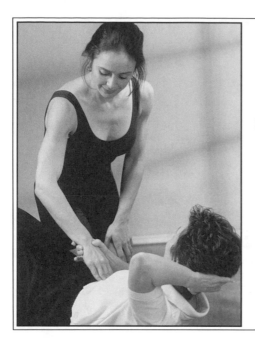

■ *5.28 Allowing the exerciser to feel your abdominal muscles as you explain which muscles are working and their order of contraction is an effective way to help her understand and duplicate the movements.*

Oblique Twist 4

When working the obliques during a side crunch, many exercisers fail to engage the rectus abdominis before the twist. Some exercisers simply roll to one side onto the opposite shoulder to twist the obliques. To correct this, palpate the rectus abdominis to feel for the initiation of the contraction; then feel the obliques with your other hand to make sure they are engaged. Follow through with your fingers tracing the contraction down diagonally to the end of the movement. This technique is particularly helpful to the beginner who does not understand how to perform an abdominal crunch with a twist correctly.

Delaying the Effects of Muscle Fatigue 4

If you want your exerciser to hold a contraction, encourage her to "hold on" and "squeeze tighter" as you palpate the muscle at the peak of the crunch. This may recruit additional muscle fibers to delay fatigue.

How Long Will It Take to Learn?

Here and in previous chapters you have been exposed to a great deal of information, and you may be feeling overwhelmed. In fact, you may be wondering how we could claim that STT is so simple! But don't let this stop you from trying. Bear in mind that each of us learns best through practice and feedback. Begin slowly and experiment using only the portions of the technique you feel comfortable with. You'll be surprised how easily you learn the language of touch.

I suggest that you focus on only one muscle group per training session. As you integrate STT into your training program, rely on your exercisers to let you know what works and what doesn't. I do that to this day. I might ask, "Did that touch help you stay focused?" or "Did my touch help you complete those extra three reps?"

Remember that muscle boundaries are not well defined; there will be slight differences in each individual. Some trial and error may be required to obtain the desired effect.

Finally, you will learn more quickly if you practice your touch techniques on yourself. Using self-touch when I train helps keep me totally focused and working at full capacity. Although I can touch only certain muscles during my own workout, I still enjoy many of the same benefits I provide my exercisers through touch training.

You will undoubtedly experience some initial awkwardness, but your confidence will build quickly as you see and feel your exercisers responding positively to your touch. The more you use STT, the more comfortable and creative you will become with it and the greater your rewards will be.

Summary

In this chapter we have demonstrated how the techniques and procedures discussed in chapters 3 and 4 can be integrated into an exercise session. We have focused on four muscles, but the techniques can easily be adapted to any other muscle and to various types of exercise equipment. Our discussion has been organized around the four basic components of the STT exercise session: warm-up and observation, explanation, evaluation, and instruction/feedback. We recommend that you pay special attention to body alignment, initiation, bilateral symmetry, unwanted tension, and the onset of fatigue. Remember that your selection of hand techniques depends on your hand size in relation to your exerciser's muscle size. It won't take you long to perfect hand techniques that work best for both you and your exerciser.

CHAPTER *Six*

WINNING HANDS DOWN

Using STT to Improve Sport Performance

> Where there is an open mind
> there will always be a frontier.
>
> Charles F. Kettering (1954)

Well, there you have it. You have the concept and the tools you need to put STT to use for immediate results. If the enhancement of strength and function were the only purposes for using our touch training technique, we would feel justified in having written this book. But there is another purpose that with further research and investigation may prove to be the most important. That purpose is to improve muscular coordination during the performance of various sport skills.

Coordination is the ability to contract muscles in the correct sequence and with appropriate force. When someone is performing a skill, he is said to be coordinated if his movements look "smooth," whereas he is called uncoordinated if his movements look "awkward." The only way to develop coordination is through practice and accompanying feedback. We are all familiar with the adage "practice makes perfect." But, actually, practice alone does not lead to improved skill. The adage should be, "practice with correct feedback makes perfect." It has been shown repeatedly that skill improves when correct feedback is provided after a practice trial. After the amount of practice, feedback is considered the most important factor in a practice session. STT provides a rich source of feedback about both the location and the amount of muscle activity. Along with serving as a source of information after a practice trial, STT can also provide *feedforward* information. It follows then that STT, in addition to its value in the weightroom, could be used to teach sport skills.

Using STT to Provide Feedback Information

After a practice, the coach or trainer should provide feedback to the athlete about technique and/or the outcome of the skill. Information about technique is called *knowledge of performance* (KP), whereas information about the outcome of the skill is called *knowledge of results* (KR). The most effective use of STT is in providing KP.

As we now know, the skin is an uncommon but very useful source of feedback. Touching the skin sends a message to the brain that can signal the location of the muscle that needs to be contracted or relaxed. Touch can also provide feedback about the amount of tension that the muscle is producing. For example, I once monitored the working muscles of a young college athlete on the rowing team. Seated behind him, and using STT to evaluate muscle tension, I found that he was using his biceps rather than his back muscles to initiate the rowing motion. On the basis of this feedback, I decided to palpate his latissimus and shoulder muscles during the rowing motion and instructed him to initiate the movement with those muscles. He was soon able to perform the movement with greater strength and increased efficiency.

After the practice session, he confided that his coach had often reminded him to "pull with the back and not with the arms," but he had not grasped its full significance. Touch showed him how to tap into an unexpected and unused source of power and energy.

Using STT to Provide Feedforward Information

Unlike feedback provided after a practice trial, *feedforward* information is supplied to your athlete before the trials begin. You can cue an exerciser as to which muscles to use to perform a skill and when to use them by touching the muscles in the order of their intended use. This helps the athlete to develop a mental picture of the movements and form a plan of action.

We believe that STT can both facilitate the contraction of a muscle and arouse the central nervous system. Either of these contributes to an increased ability to control a specific muscle at a certain time. It follows that there are obvious applications of STT in sports where the contraction (or absence of a contraction) of a muscle at just the right moment makes the difference between success and failure. The following two examples should illustrate how STT can be used to provide feedforward information.

A client of mine recently asked me to help her improve some of her tennis skills. Before practice one afternoon, I used the phantom fingers technique to palpate and stroke several muscles I knew to be important in performing the forehand drive. While doing so, I instructed her to focus her attention on those muscles and their proper sequencing pattern. My goal was for her to develop a mental picture of the sequence of muscle contractions she needed to perform the movement. As expected, her technique improved appreciably. She also reported an improvement in the accuracy of her shots and an increased awareness of her limbs during the execution of her strokes.

Consider another example—a college student named Krista worked for me several years ago as a typist. She was a goalie for her university's soccer team. One day we were talking about her inability to maintain quickness in her leaps and dives for the duration of an entire soccer match. Apparently, fatigue was causing her to miss many of the same kind of shots that she had been able to stop early in the match. Her coach had been working with her, but she was unable to transfer his words into action. She had been using the incorrect form for so long while fatigued that to change was difficult. I decided to use STT to redirect her focus to her gluteal muscles and instructed her to initiate her lateral movements with these muscles rather than with her lower legs. Using the palpation/squeeze method, I was able to teach her to move from her glutes. Then I showed her how to use phantom fingers to develop a mental picture of the contraction sequence. Later, during her games, she used self-touch to focus her attention on initiating her dives and leaps with her glutes. She quickly adapted her form and was able to decrease her fatigue and improve her quickness while performing these skills.

Improved Function for Elite Athletes

The value of STT has recently been recognized by top health professionals involved in the training and treatment of elite athletes. Cindy Bailey, a well-known Los Angeles physical therapist who has treated such athletes as Jackie Joyner-Kersee, Byron Scott, Florence Griffith, Willie Banks, and Tracy Austin, had this to say about STT:

Strength training, which is exercise specific, only strengthens the muscles to perform certain motions. In order to have it translate into functional activities, you must put the athlete into the functional activity position and teach them to use their new strength functionally. This can best be accomplished by touching those muscle groups not only during strength training, but also during functional training. T.O.U.C.H. training "turns on" the muscle and provides the leap into improved function.

Using STT to Teach Sport Skills to People With Disabilities

Another promising application of STT is with people who have disabilities or special needs. A person who is visually impaired, for instance, would probably benefit from using STT to improve either functional or sport-related motor skills. A few years ago, Oscar and I were asked to help prepare a group of teenagers with visual impairments for the Braille Track and Field Olympics. We had been working as volunteers at the Braille Institute, helping young people to improve their strength and fitness. One week before the state championships, Armando, a 17-year-old who was blind, decided that he wanted to compete in the shot put, which was for him a new event. One of the other trainers tried to explain the correct technique to him and moved his arms through the motion of the put. Armando practiced several times and had a best throw of 10 feet. However, it was clear that he did not fully understand the technique. I asked the trainer if I could work with Armando. While providing verbal instruction, I touched those body parts necessary to perform the put, beginning with the foot placement, then the hip, and finally the shoulders and upper back. After several practice puts, he exclaimed, "Now, I get it!" His next throw went 30 feet.

These and similar experiences and reports from coaches and trainers give us good reason to believe that STT has many applications outside the weightroom. As more trainers and coaches begin to adopt STT into their training programs, additional benefits will no doubt emerge. We are certain that touch training will become at least as important to sport coaches as it is currently to strength coaches.

Keep in Touch

We hope you have enjoyed this introduction to Systematic T.O.U.C.H. Training^{SM}. We wanted this book not only to provide you with a new and exciting way to train, but also to stimulate your intellectual curiosity so you will want to use your own creative talents as you apply STT's wide range of possibilities and applications. Trainers who have already incorporated STT into their training programs have found the method invaluable in guiding exercisers to greater levels of health, fitness, and athletic skill. We hope that you will enjoy the same results with this technique and that you'll keep us informed about your successes and also about any problems you encounter. If you have questions or comments, we would love to hear from you. Please write us at

P.O. Box 1764
Santa Monica, California 90406-1764

A SUPPLEMENTAL GUIDE TO T.O.U.C.H. TRAINING^{SM} TECHNIQUES[*]^{**}

MUSCLE CATEGORY I: SMALL ROUND

1 SEATED, ONE-ARM CONCENTRATION CURLS

BICEPS

Origin: scapula and humerus

Insertion: radius and ulna

Method used for:
Eval: MT
Stim: S,P,P/S,C
Relax: MT
Guide: S,W

Notes
1. Perfect exercise to teach self-touch techniques. Easy access to muscle. Both trainer and exerciser can evaluate contraction at once.
2. Touch point on inner thigh where elbow will rest. Exerciser should keep this point of contact throughout.
3. Touch sternum firmly; then ask exerciser to lift into that touch to avoid leaning backward to "cheat the weight up."
4. Stroke down the length of the muscle on the lowering phase. "Walk" up the muscle on lift and palpate point of muscle "tie in" as you encourage the squeeze to peak contraction.

---

*Abbreviations: vert = vertebrae; eval = evaluation; stim = stimulation; TTR = touch-to-relax; guide = guiding the movement; MT = maintained touch; S = stroking; W = walking; P = palpation; P/S = palpation/squeeze; KE = knife-edge; C = cupping; PF = phantom fingers

**The hand methods recommended in this chart were selected because they are appropriate for the exercise examples offered. Given a different exercise, other hand methods and touch cues might be equally as effective for the particular body part. The suggestions offered in the notes should be employed only when you deem them appropriate depending upon the needs of the individual exerciser.

TRICEPS

2   TRICEPS PRESS-DOWN

Origin: scapula and humerus

Insertion: ulna

Method used for:
Eval: MT
Stim: S,P,P/S
Relax: MT
Guide: S

Notes   1. Try not to touch the exerciser's biceps during the movement.
2. Standing behind the exerciser, place two fingers on inside edge of elbows and instruct him or her to keep elbows against your fingers while pressing the bar outward in a wide semicircle.
3. Use S and/or P/S from elbow to shoulder on the press-down and slightly lighter stroking in the opposite direction on the upward stretch.

TRICEPS

3   TRICEPS KICKBACKS

Origin: scapula and humerus

Insertion: ulna

Method used for:
Eval: MT
Stim: S,P,P/S
Relax: MT
Guide: S

Notes   1. See comments for the triceps press-down.
2. Use three or four fingers to palpate the long head of the triceps, and then ask exerciser to use his arm to press your fingers against his side.
3. Use palpation to stimulate posterior delt as you instruct your exerciser to stabilize the arm by moving it slightly upward and back into the shoulder joint during the kickback.
4. Use MT to feel for peak contraction in the triceps as opposed to merely a locked elbow joint.

BRACHIORADIALIS

4   WRIST CURLS AND EXTENSIONS

Origin: lateral humerus

Insertion: distal end of radius

Method used for:
Eval: MT
Stim: S,P
Relax: MT
Guide: S

Notes   1. With two or three fingers, palpate and/or stroke the forearm during flexion and extension.
2. Use MT to feel for the elongation and stretch in the muscle, not just a dropping of the weight at the wrist.

ANTERIOR DELTOIDS

5   FORWARD DUMBBELL RAISES

Origin: clavicle and scapula

Insertion: humerus

Method used for:
Eval: MT
Stim: P
Relax: MT
Guide: P,S

Notes   1. Standing behind exerciser, palpate anterior delts to focus attention and stimulate these muscles.
2. Using MT at midpoint in exercise, evaluate to ensure that inward rotation ("pouring") occurs at shoulder and not wrist.
3. To keep upper traps from becoming overinvolved, use TTR.

MIDDLE DELTOIDS

6   LATERAL DUMBBELL RAISES

Origin: clavicle and scapula

Insertion: humerus

Method used for:
Eval: MT
Stim: S,P,P/S,C
Relax: MT
Guide: S

Notes   1. See notes for anterior delts.
2. Use P/S on the middle delts during upward lift and stroke delts outward toward the elbows on the downward movement.
3. Touch elbows before and occasionally during lift as you remind exerciser to lead with the elbows, not the hands.
4. Touch sternum as you instruct exerciser to keep his or her body weight shifted forward over the balls of the feet.

POSTERIOR DELTOIDS

7 REAR DELTOID FLYS

Origin: clavicle and scapula

Insertion: humerus

Method used for:
Eval: MT
Stim: P
Relax: MT
Guide: S,P

Notes 1. Palpate posterior delts during lift to focus attention and stimulate these muscles.
2. Touch elbows, then ears, and ask the exerciser to draw an imaginary straight line between the two points as he or she leads the lift with elbows.

GASTROCNEMIUS

8 HEEL RAISES

Origin: posterior femur

Insertion: calcaneus

Method used for:
Eval: MT,P/S
Stim: S,P,P/S,C
Relax: MT
Guide: S,KE

Notes 1. Try working with shoes off. Firmly palpate exerciser's arch with two or three fingers to encourage higher lift.
2. Using P/S stimulate full length of gastroc on medial and lateral sides.
3. Stroke full length of gastroc downward to back of ankle to encourage an elongated stretch.

MUSCLE CATEGORY II: LARGE ROUND

PECTORALS

9 BENCH PRESS

Origin: clavicle, sternum, rib cartilage
Insertion: humerus

Method used for:
Eval: MT
Stim: S,P
Relax: MT
Guide: S,W,KE

Notes 1. Before beginning, palpate abdominals and remind exerciser to maintain gentle pelvic tilt and abdominal contraction during bench press.
2. Stroke outward on diagonal from sternum to shoulders during lowering of barbell; use walking method inward along same path during lift.
3. Employ KE method along length of the sternum to provide goal for exerciser as he or she rounds pecs at peak of contractions.

10   INCLINE FLYS

PECTORALS

Origin: clavicle, sternum,
          rib cartilage
Insertion: humerus

Method used for:
Eval: MT,P
Stim: S,P
Relax: MT
Guide: S,W,KE

Notes   1. See notes for bench press.
         2. Touch tips of elbows as you instruct exerciser to keep elbows
            back and lifted away from torso.
         3. Use MT to evaluate for full and safe stretch at bottom of
            movement.
         4. Apply TTR on upper traps.

11   STEP BACK LUNGE

GLUTEALS

Origin: ilium and sacrum

Insertion: femur

Method used for:
Eval: MT
Stim: P
Relax: MT
Guide: P

Notes   1. Using two fingers held closely together, palpate the lower
            gluteus maximus, while the front thigh is parallel to the
            ground. Instruct your exerciser to press forward heel
            down as he or she moves into lifting phase.

12   REVERSE HYPEREXTENSION

GLUTEALS

Origin: ilium and sacrum

Insertion: femur

Method used for:
Eval: MT,P
Stim:P
Relax: MT
Guide: P

Notes   1. Using two fingers held closely together, palpate the upper
            borders of the gluteals as you instruct exerciser to squeeze
            the muscle for peak contraction.
         2. Stroke spinal erectors in a downward motion as legs are low-
            ered for the eccentric contraction. Instruct exerciser to elon-
            gate these muscles during the lowering phase.

HAMSTRINGS

13   LEG CURL (MACHINE)

Origin: ischium and femur

Insertion: fibula and tibia

Method used for:
Eval: MT,P
Stim: S,P,P/S
Relax: MT
Guide: S,P,P/S

Notes
1. Touch hip bones as you instruct exerciser to press pelvis to the bench.
2. When using MT, S, P, or P/S on the hamstrings, a moderate to firm touch is required, as this is a large muscle that doesn't respond well to a light touch.
3. Use stroking and palpation along the length of the muscle to ensure that the hamstrings have gone through a full range of motion.

HAMSTRINGS

14   STANDING SINGLE LEG CURL

Origin: ischium and femur

Insertion: fibula and tibia

Method used for:
Eval: MT,P
Stim: S,P,P/S
Relax: MT
Guide: S,P,KE

Notes
1. See notes for leg curl (machine).
2. Palpate the exerciser's abdominals slightly below the navel while instructing him or her to contract abdominals and to gently press hip bones forward (slight pelvic tilt) to stabilize the back.

QUADRICEPS

15   BARBELL BACK SQUAT

Origin: femur and ilium

Insertion: patella and tibia

Method used for:
Eval: inappropriate
Stim: PF
Relax: MT
Guide: inappropriate

Notes
1. Use phantom fingers (PF) to firmly and quickly stroke the quads just prior to the lifting of the barbell onto the shoulders. Instruct exerciser to focus on the location of the touch and to recall it during the movement.

ABDOMINALS

16 SUPINE, LATERAL FLEXION, SEMICIRCLES

Origin: anterior pelvis

Insertion: lower rib cage

Method used for:
Eval: MT,P
Stim: S,P,P/S
Relax: MT
Guide: S

Notes
1. Have exerciser assume pelvic tilt; place thumb and middle finger of one hand on "upper" and "lower" abs; bring finger and thumb together slowly as you instruct exerciser to contract abdominals. Using flat hand, MT, place both hands on rib cage and instruct exerciser to close down ribs.
2. Just prior to and during lateral movement, palpate the obliques and rectus abdominis on the side toward which the exerciser is moving.
3. Use TTR to release tension in the traps.

MUSCLE CATEGORY III: LARGE FLAT

LATISSIMUS DORSI

17 ONE-ARM ROW

Origin: thoracic and lumbar
 vertebrae and ilium

Insertion: anterior humerus

Method used for:
Eval: MT
Stim: P,S
Relax: MT
Guide: S

Notes
1. Palpate sternum and both "hipbones" as you remind exerciser to keep torso parallel to the floor.
2. Use MT to determine that the lift originates with the back muscles, not the arm.
3. Use P or S to stimulate the middle and lower traps and lats during the lift.
4. Touch elbow and hip and instruct exerciser to draw elbow upward and back alongside of body toward touch point on hip.

#18   HYPEREXTENSION (MACHINE)

SPINAL ERECTORS

Origin: iliac crest, sacrum, and lumbar vertebrae
Insertion: lumbar to cervical vertebrae and ribs

Method used for:
Eval: MT,P
Stim: P,S
Relax: MT
Guide: S

Notes   1. Using two or three fingers held firmly together, palpate glutes and hams just prior to the lift to evaluate for initiation in these muscles.
2. Stroke erectors upward at the beginning of both the lifting and lowering phases while instructing exerciser to "elongate spine."
3. Palpate erectors to stimulate contraction.

#19   GOOD MORNINGS

SPINAL ERECTORS

Origin: iliac crest, sacrum, and lumbar vertebrae
Insertion: lumbar to cervical vertebrae and ribs

Method used for:
Eval: MT
Stim: P,S
Relax: MT
Guide: S

Notes   1. Just prior to bending forward: a) Instruct exerciser to keep rib cage lifted as you palpate rhomboids and upper back muscles (remind exerciser to maintain arch in his or her back); b) palpate lower abdominals and instruct exerciser to contract for stabilization; and c) touch lightly the back of the knees as you instruct exerciser to keep knees slightly bent.

#20   NARROW GRIP UPRIGHT ROWS

UPPER TRAPEZIUS

Origin: occipital bone, cervical and thoracic vertebrae
Insertion: clavicle and scapula

Method used for:
Eval: MT
Stim: P
Relax: MT
Guide: S,P

Notes   1. Standing behind exerciser, palpate upper traps during lift. Then stroke away from the neck and over the shoulders during controlled downward motion.
2. Touching the elbows helps exerciser focus and guide the lift.
3. Standing in front of your exerciser, touch sternum to remind him or her not to lean away from the bar.

MIDDLE & LOWER TRAPEZIUS

#**21**   BENT-OVER BARBELL ROWS

Origin: occipital bone, cervical
  and thoracic vertebrae
Insertion: clavicle and scapula

Method used for:
Eval: MT
Stim: P,S
Relax: MT
Guide: S,W

Notes   1. Palpate and/or stroke middle and lower traps to stimulate these muscles.
   2. Standing to the side of the exerciser, touch inside borders of scapula (using two fingers on each side) as you encourage full stretch on the downward movement.

TENSOR FASCIAE LATAE (ABDUCTORS)

#**22**   WEIGHTED, SIDE-LYING SINGLE LEG RAISE

Origin: ilium

Insertion: tibia

Method used for:
Eval: MT
Stim: S,P,P/S
Relax: MT
Guide: S,P

Notes   1. To place exerciser in proper body alignment, ask exerciser to initiate a gentle pelvic tilt and slightly squeeze glutes together as you "smooth down" tailbone using S with heel of palm. Apply thumb and middle finger to lower rib cage with light P/S on exhalation to aid closure of rib cage.
   2. Palpate lower abdominals to verify contraction.
   3. Touch iliac crest and tell exerciser not to raise working leg above hip level.
   4. Palpate tensor fasciae latae and gluteus medius before and during the leg lift to focus attention on these muscles.

ADDUCTORS

#**23**   WEIGHTED, SIDE-LYING SINGLE LEG RAISE

Origin: pubic bone

Insertion: femur

Method used for:
Eval: MT
Stim: S,P
Relax: MT,P
Guide: S,P,W

Notes   1. With stationary leg supported on a bench, use MT on the adductors of the working leg during the lift to evaluate muscle involvement. Palpate to stimulate any "lazy" areas.
   2. Touch medial side of instep on working leg as you instruct exerciser to lift leg from point of touch upward to underside of bench pad.

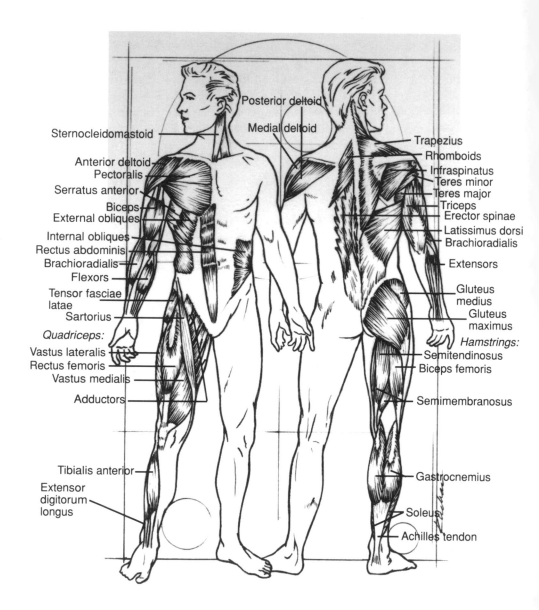

Sternocleidomastoid

Anterior deltoid
Pectoralis
Serratus anterior
Biceps
External obliques
Internal obliques
Rectus abdominis
Brachioradialis
Flexors
Tensor fasciae latae
Sartorius
Quadriceps:
Vastus lateralis
Rectus femoris
Vastus medialis
Adductors

Tibialis anterior
Extensor digitorum longus

Posterior deltoid
Medial deltoid

Trapezius
Rhomboids
Infraspinatus
Teres minor
Teres major
Triceps
Erector spinae
Latissimus dorsi
Brachioradialis
Extensors
Gluteus medius
Gluteus maximus
Hamstrings:
Semitendinosus
Biceps femoris
Semimembranosus
Gastrocnemius
Soleus
Achilles tendon

BIBLIOGRAPHY

Bach-y-Rita, P. (1972). *Brain mechanisms in sensory substitution.* New York: Academic Press.

Basmajian, J.V. (1963). Control and training of individual motor units. *Science,* **141,** 44.

Basmajian, J.V. (1978). *Therapeutic exercise* (3rd ed.). Baltimore: Williams & Wilkins.

Basmajian, J.V., & DeLuca, C.J. (1985). *Muscles alive* (5th ed.). Baltimore: Williams & Wilkins.

Burke, R.E., Jankowitz, H., & Ten Bruggencate, E. (1970). A comparison of peripheral and central synaptic input to slow and fast twitch motor units of triceps surae. *Journal of Physiology,* **207,** 709-732.

Burke, R.E., Levine, D.N., Tsairis, P., & Zajac, F.E. (1973). Physiological types and histochemical profiles in motor units of the cat gastrocnemius. *Journal of Physiology,* **234,** 723-748.

Capute, A.J., Accordo, P.J., Vining, E.P.G., Rubenstein, J.E., & Harryman, S. (1978). Primitive reflex profile. *Monographs in developmental paediatrics,* Vol. 1. Baltimore: University Park Press.

Duncan, P.W., & Badke, M.B. (Eds.) (1978). *Stroke rehabilitation: The recovery of motor control.* Chicago: Yearbook Medical Publishers.

Geldard, F.A. (1961). Cutaneous channels of communication. In W.A. Rosenblith (Ed.), *Sensory communication.* Cambridge, MA: MIT Press.

Gordon, G. (1978). *Active touch.* New York: Pergamon Press.

Griffin, J.W. (1974). Use of proprioceptive stimuli in therapeutic exercise. *Physical Therapy,* **54,** 1072-1079.

Hagbarth, K.-E. (1978). Excitatory and inhibitory skin areas for flexor and extensor motoneurons. In O.D. Payton, S. Hirt, & R. Newton (Eds.), *Scientific Basis for Neurophysiologic Approaches to Therapeutic Exercise: An Anthology.* Philadelphia: F.A. Davies Co.

Jenkins, W.M., Merzenich, M.M., Ochs, M.T., Allard, T., & Guic-Robles, E. (1981). Functional reorganization of primary somatosensory cortex in adult owl monkeys after behaviorally controlled tactile stimulation. *Journal of Neurophysiology,* **63**(1), 82-104.

Johnstone, M. (1987). *Restoration of motor function in the stroke patient: A physiotherapist's approach* (3rd ed.). London: Churchill Livingstone.

Masakado, Y., Kamen, G., & De Luca, C.J. (1991). Effects of percutaneous stimulation on motor unit firing behavior in man. *Experimental Brain Research*, **86**, 426-432.

McGlown, D.J. (1990). *Developmental reflexive rehabilitation*. London: Taylor & Francis, Ltd.

Melzack, R., & Wall, P.D. (1983). *The challenge of pain*. New York: Basic Books.

Montagu, A. (1986). *Touching: The human significance of the skin*. New York: Harper & Row.

Mountcastle, V.B. (1975). The view from within: Pathways to the study of perception. *Johns-Hopkins Medical Journal*, **136**, 109-131.

Mulder, T. (1985). *The learning of motor control following brain damage: Experimental and clinical studies*. Lisse, Netherlands: Swess & Zeitlinger.

Norsell, U. (1980). Behavioral studies of the somatosensory system. *Physiological Reviews*, **60**(2), 327-354.

Rood, M.S. (1954). Neurophysiological reactions as a basis for physical therapy. *Physical Therapy Review*, **34**, 444.

Rood, M.S. (1956). Neurophysiological mechanisms utilized in the treatment of neuromuscular dysfunction. *American Journal of Occupational Therapy*, **10**, 220.

Sale, D.G. (1988). Neural adaptations to resistance training. *Medicine and Science in Sports and Exercise*, **20**, 135.

Schmidt, R.A. (1988). *Motor control and learning* (2nd ed.). Champaign, IL: Human Kinetics.

Sherrick, C.E. (1982). Cutaneous communication. In W.D. Neff (Ed.), *Contributions to Sensory Physiology* (Vol. 6). New York: Academic Press.

Stein, R.B., & Capaday, C. (1988). The modulation of human reflexes during functional motor tasks. *Trends in Neuroscience*, **11**, 17.

Wall, J.T. (1988). Variable organization in cortical maps of the skin as an indication of the lifelong adaptive capacities of circuits in the mammalian brain. *Trends in Neuroscience*, **11**(12), 549-557.

Whitsel, B.L., Favorov, O.V., Tommerdahl, M., Diamond, M.E., Juliano, S.L., & Kelly, D.G. (1989). Dynamic processes governing the somatosensory cortical response to natural stimulation. In J.S. Lund (Ed.), *Sensory Processing in the Mammalian Brain*. New York: Academic Press.

Yerkes, R.M., & Dodson, J.D. (1908). The relationship of strength of stimulus to rapidity of habit formation. *Journal of Comparative Neurology and Psychology*, **18**, 459-482.

Supplemental Reading

Clemente, C.D. (1987). *Anatomy: A regional atlas of the human body* (3rd ed.). Malvern, PA: Lea & Febiger.

Hay, J.G., & Reid, J.G. (1988). *The anatomical and mechanical basis of human motion.* Englewood Cliffs, NJ: Prentice-Hall.

Kreighbaum, E., & Barthels, K.M. (1985). *Biomechanics.* New York: Macmillan.

Luttgens, K., & Wells, K.F. (1989). *Kinesiology* (7th ed.). Dubuque, IA: William C. Brown.

Rasch, P.J. (1989). *Kinesiology and applied anatomy.* Malvern, PA: Lea & Febiger.

INDEX

ABOUT THE AUTHORS

Beth Rothenberg has been using Systematic T.O.U.C.H. Training to successfully train her clients since she first became a personal fitness trainer more than 20 years ago. She has shared STT with leading coaches, trainers, and elite athletes, and has used the technique to help train visually-impaired teenagers at the Braille Institute.

Beth lectures nationally to fitness professionals on training techniques and motivation. She is an instructor for the award-winning UCLA Extension Fitness Instructor Certificate Program and for the Advanced Specialty Certificate Program for personal fitness trainers. She is also certified as a health/fitness instructor by the American College of Sports Medicine (ACSM).

Oscar Rothenberg is an attorney who has specialized in the medical/legal field for 30 years. He lectures on legal and ethical issues pertaining to fitness professionals and was a member of the item writing committee for the American Council on Exercise Personal Trainer Certification Exam. As co-author of *Touch Training for Strength*, he was instrumental in organizing and systematizing the method of Systematic T.O.U.C.H. Training.

The Rothenbergs live in Santa Monica, California. They spend most of their leisure time enjoying their secluded mountain retreat in northern California.

For workshops and seminars presented by the authors on the practical application of the principles outlined in this book, please call or write

STT Workshops and Seminars
Post Office Box 1764
Santa Monica, California 90406-1764
(310) 454-7648   FAX (310) 459-6626

STT Workshops and Seminars offer approved CEU credit for sport and fitness professionals from leading industry organizations.